MEL BAY PRESENTS

MODERN GUITAR METHOD GRADE 1

AUTHOR'S NOTE

GRADE ONE

PRESENTS BASIC ELEMENTARY THEORY, ETUDES, SOLOS, DUETS, AND TECHNICAL STUDIES FOR THE BEGINNER IN THE KEYS OF C, A MINOR, G AND E MINOR.

THE TEACHER SHOULD ACCOMPANY THE STUDENT IN THE DUETS REVERSING THE PARTS WITH THE PUPIL.

SUGGESTED SUPPLEMENTS TO THE MEL BAY MODERN GUITAR METHOD—VOL. 1

CHORD PLAYING

1. Fun with Strums—Guitar
2. EZ Way Pick & Strum Solos
3. EZ Way Country Style Guitar Solos

SOLO PLAYING

1. Solo Folio #1—Great Solo Favorites
2. EZ Way Rock Guitar Solos
3. EZ Way Bluegrass Guitar Solos
4. EZ Way Boogie & Blues Guitar Solos

TECHNIQUE

1. Guitar Technic

TUNING

1. EZ Way to Tune Guitars

THE CORRECT WAY TO HOLD THE GUITAR

THIS IS THE PICK

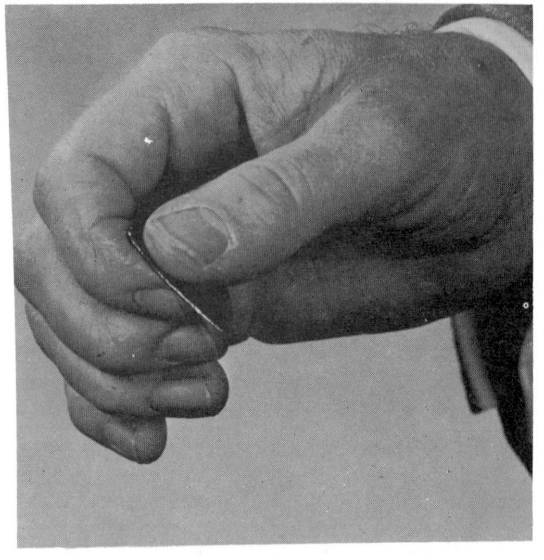

HOLD IT IN THIS MANNER
FIRMLY BETWEEN THE THUMB
AND FIRST FINGER.

THE LEFT HAND POSITION

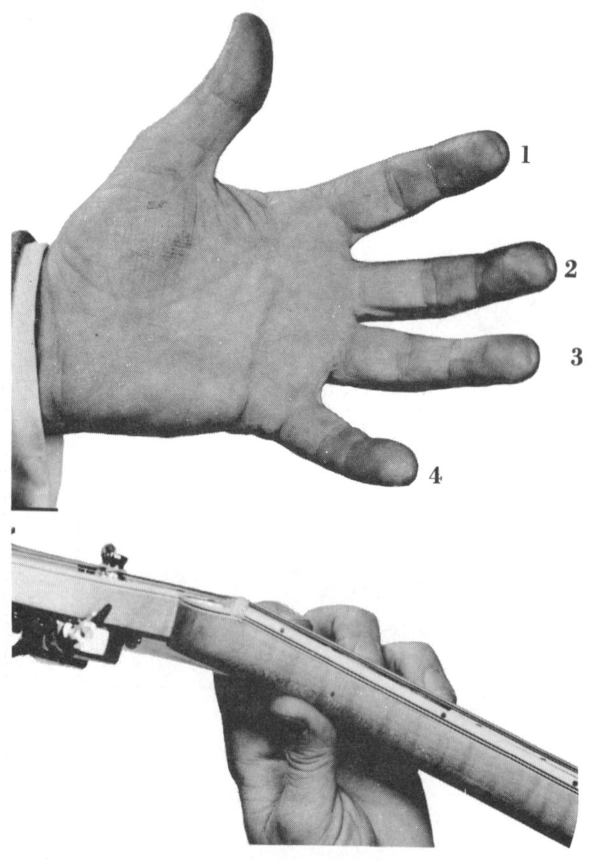

Place your fingers FIRMLY on the strings
DIRECTLY BEHIND THE FRETS.

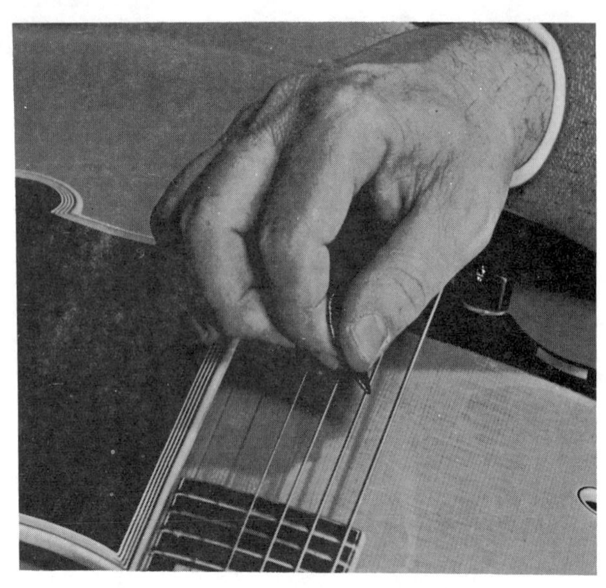

STRIKING THE STRINGS

⊓ = DOWN STROKE OF THE PICK.

TUNING THE GUITAR

The six open strings of the guitar will be of the same pitch as the six notes shown in the illustration of the piano keyboard. Note that five of the strings are below the middle C of the piano keyboard.

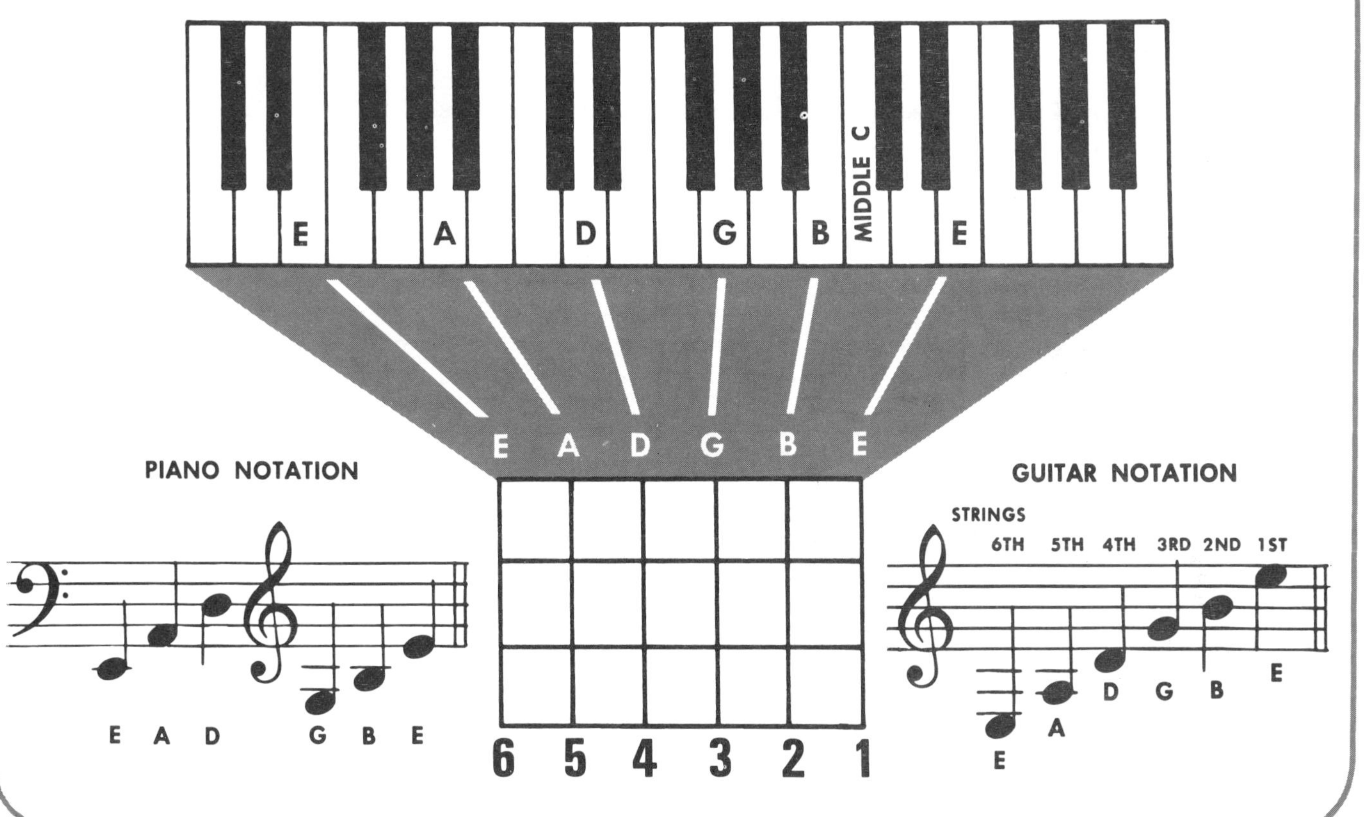

ANOTHER METHOD OF TUNING

1. Tune the 6th string in unison to the **E** or twelfth white key to the LEFT of MIDDLE C on the piano.
2. Place the finger behind the fifth fret of the 6th string. This will give you the tone or pitch of the 5th string. (**A**)
3. Place finger behind the fifth fret of the 5th string to get the pitch of the 4th string. (**D**)
4. Repeat same procedure to obtain the pitch of the 3rd string. (**G**)
5. Place finger behind the FOURTH FRET of the 3rd string to get the pitch of the 2nd string. (**B**)
6. Place finger behind the fifth fret of the 2nd string to get the pitch of the 1st string. (**E**)

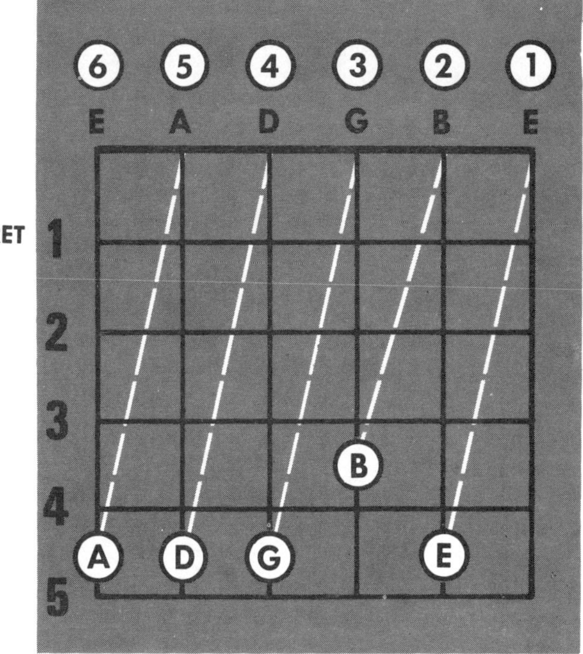

PITCH PIPES

Pitch pipes with instructions for their usage may be obtained at any music store. Each pipe will have the correct pitch of each guitar string and are recommended to be used when a piano is not available.

THE RUDIMENTS OF MUSIC

THE STAFF: Music is written on a STAFF consisting of FIVE LINES and FOUR SPACES. The lines and spaces are numbered upward as shown:

5TH LINE
4TH SPACE
4TH LINE
3RD SPACE
3RD LINE
2ND SPACE
2ND LINE
1ST SPACE
1ST LINE

THE LINES AND SPACES ARE NAMED AFTER LETTERS OF THE ALPHABET.

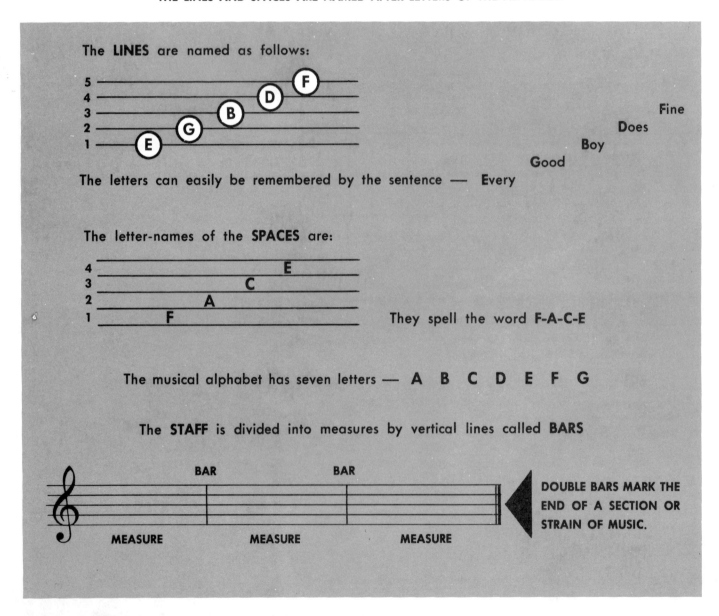

The **LINES** are named as follows:

5 F
4 D
3 B
2 G
1 E

The letters can easily be remembered by the sentence — **Every Good Boy Does Fine**

The letter-names of the **SPACES** are:

4 E
3 C
2 A
1 F

They spell the word **F-A-C-E**

The musical alphabet has seven letters — **A B C D E F G**

The **STAFF** is divided into measures by vertical lines called **BARS**

BAR BAR

MEASURE MEASURE MEASURE

DOUBLE BARS MARK THE END OF A SECTION OR STRAIN OF MUSIC.

THE CLEF:

THIS SIGN IS THE TREBLE OR G CLEF.

ALL GUITAR MUSIC WILL BE WRITTEN IN THIS CLEF.

THE SECOND LINE OF THE TREBLE CLEF IS KNOWN AS THE G LINE. MANY PEOPLE CALL THE TREBLE CLEF THE G CLEF BECAUSE IT CIRCLES AROUND THE G LINE.

NOTES:

THIS IS A NOTE:

A NOTE HAS THREE PARTS. THEY ARE

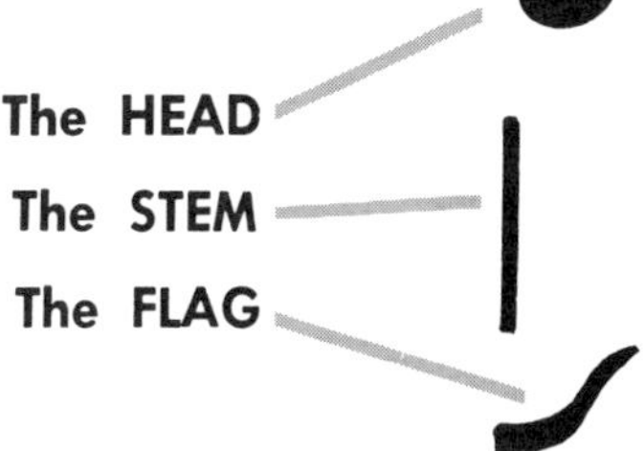

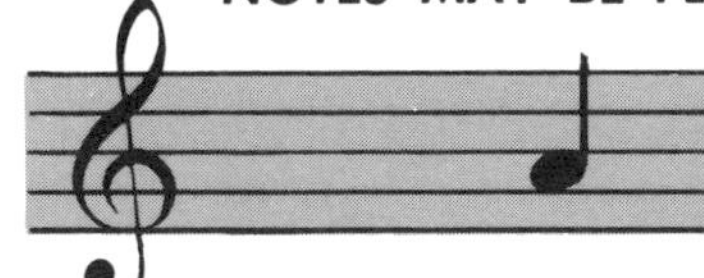

NOTES MAY BE PLACED IN THE STAFF, ABOVE THE STAFF,

AND BELOW THE STAFF.

A note will bear the name of the line or space it occupies on the staff.

The location of a note in, above or below the staff will indicate the Pitch.

PITCH: the height or depth of a tone.

TONE: a musical sound.

TYPES OF NOTES

THE TYPE OF NOTE WILL INDICATE THE LENGTH OF ITS SOUND.

THIS IS A WHOLE NOTE.
THE HEAD IS HOLLOW.
IT DOES NOT HAVE A STEM.

= 4 BEATS
A WHOLE-NOTE WILL RECEIVE FOUR BEATS OR COUNTS.

THIS IS A HALF NOTE
THE HEAD IS HOLLOW.
IT HAS A STEM.

= 2 BEATS
A HALF-NOTE WILL RECEIVE TWO BEATS OR COUNTS.

THIS IS A QUARTER NOTE
THE HEAD IS SOLID.
IT HAS A STEM.

= 1 BEAT
A QUARTER NOTE WILL RECEIVE ONE BEAT OR COUNT.

THIS IS AN EIGHTH NOTE
THE HEAD IS SOLID.
IT HAS A STEM AND A FLAG.

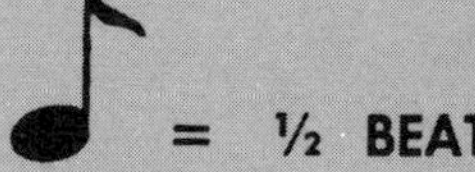

= ½ BEAT
AN EIGHTH-NOTE WILL RECEIVE ONE-HALF BEAT OR COUNT. (2 FOR 1 BEAT)

RESTS:

A REST is a sign used to designate a period of silence.

This period of silence will be of the same duration of time as the note to which it corresponds.

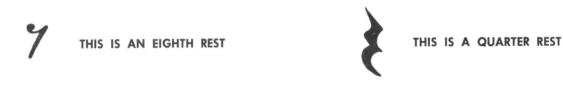

THIS IS A HALF REST. NOTE THAT IT LAYS ON THE LINE.

THIS IS A WHOLE REST. NOTE THAT IT HANGS DOWN FROM THE LINE.

NOTES

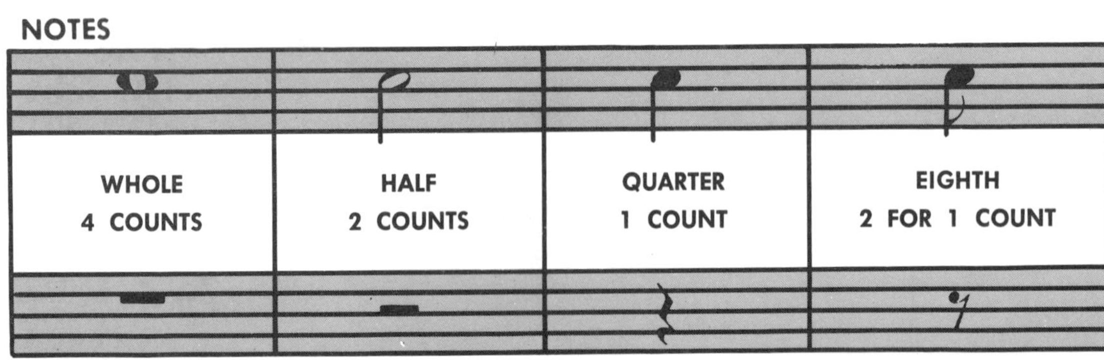

WHOLE 4 COUNTS	HALF 2 COUNTS	QUARTER 1 COUNT	EIGHTH 2 FOR 1 COUNT

RESTS

THE TIME SIGNATURE

THE ABOVE EXAMPLES ARE THE COMMON TYPES OF TIME SIGNATURES TO BE USED IN THIS BOOK.

$\frac{4}{4}$ THE TOP NUMBER INDICATES THE NUMBER OF BEATS PER MEASURE. THE BOTTOM NUMBER INDICATES THE TYPE OF NOTE RECEIVING ONE BEAT.

$\frac{4}{4}$ BEATS PER MEASURE / A QUARTER-NOTE RECEIVES ONE BEAT

SIGNIFIES SO CALLED "COMMON TIME" AND IS SIMPLY ANOTHER WAY OF DESIGNATING $\frac{4}{4}$ TIME.

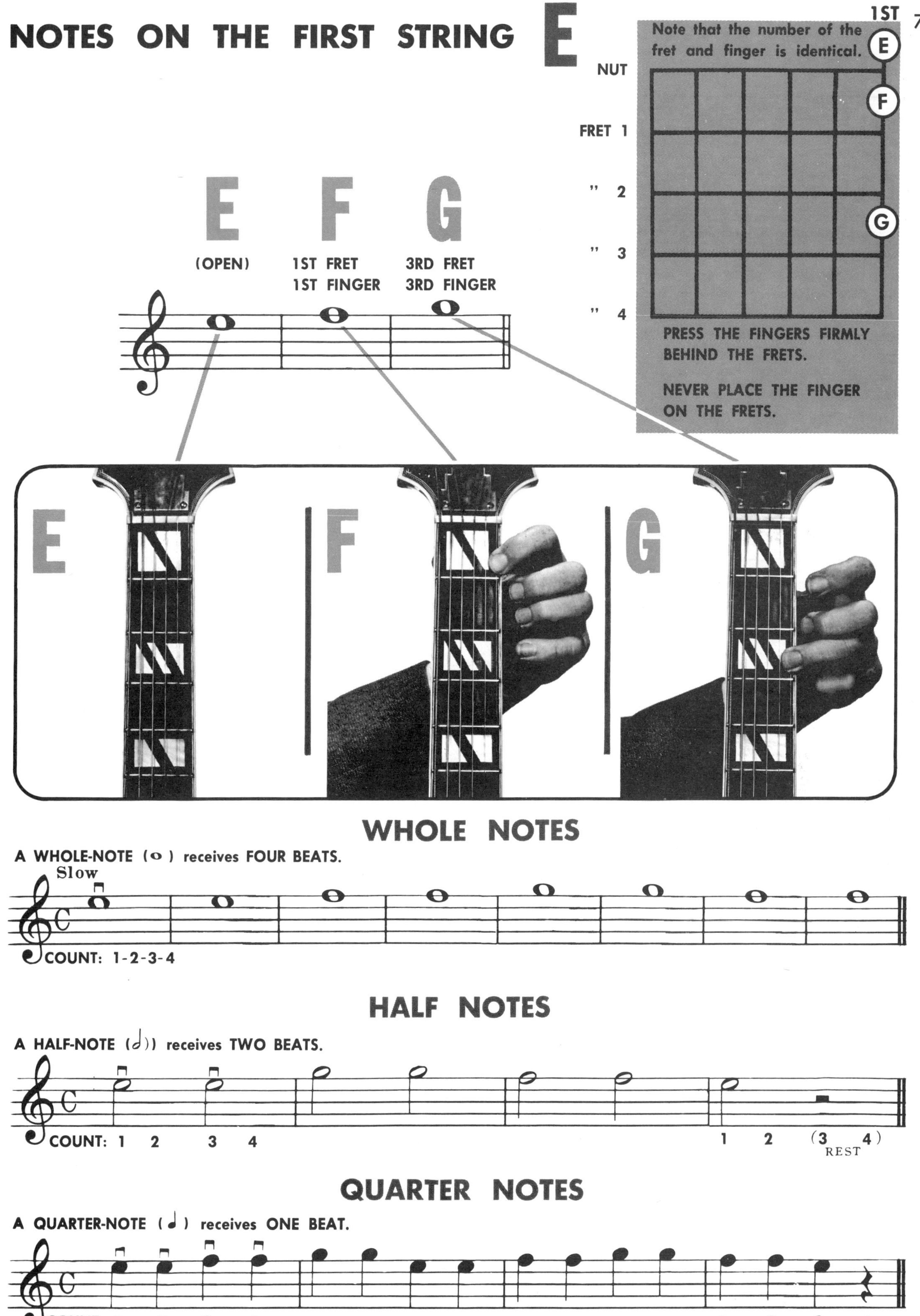
NOTES ON THE FIRST STRING E
Note that the number of the fret and finger is identical.
E
NUT
F
FRET 1
" 2
G
" 3
" 4
PRESS THE FINGERS FIRMLY BEHIND THE FRETS.
NEVER PLACE THE FINGER ON THE FRETS.
E F G
(OPEN)
1ST FRET
1ST FINGER
3RD FRET
3RD FINGER
E
F
G
WHOLE NOTES
A WHOLE-NOTE ( ) receives FOUR BEATS.
Slow
COUNT: 1-2-3-4
HALF NOTES
A HALF-NOTE ( ) receives TWO BEATS.
COUNT: 1 2 3 4
1 2 (3 4)
REST
QUARTER NOTES
A QUARTER-NOTE ( ) receives ONE BEAT.
COUNT: 1 2 3 4
1 2 3 4

1st STRING ETUDE

ETUDE NO. 2

THE MIXMASTER

NOTES ON THE FIRST STRING

(FILL IN THE BLOCKS)

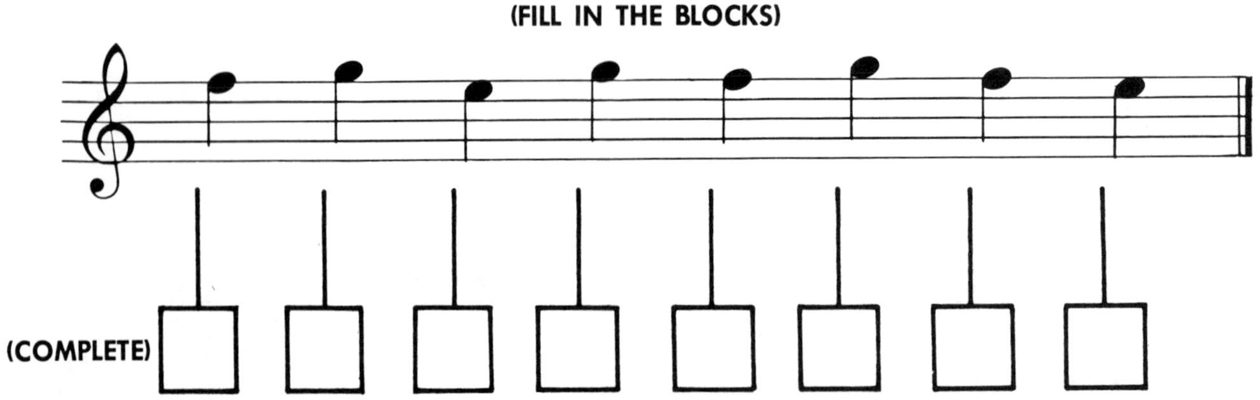

NOTES ON THE SECOND STRING B

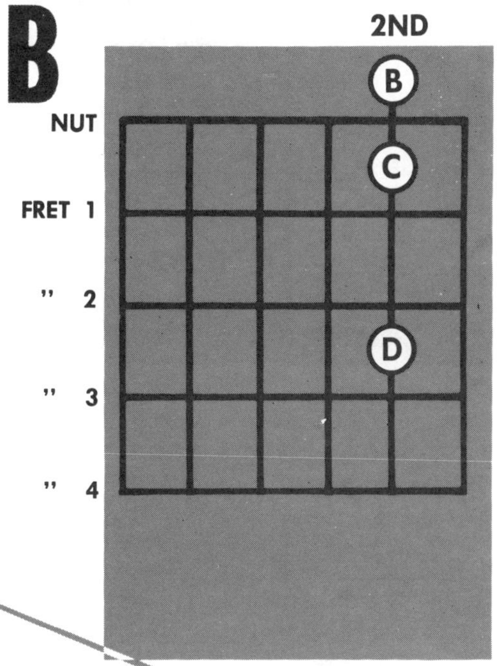

2ND

B

NUT

C

FRET 1

" 2

D

" 3

" 4

THREE NOTES ON THE 2ND STRING

B	C	D
(OPEN)	1ST FRET 1ST FINGER	3RD FRET 3RD FINGER

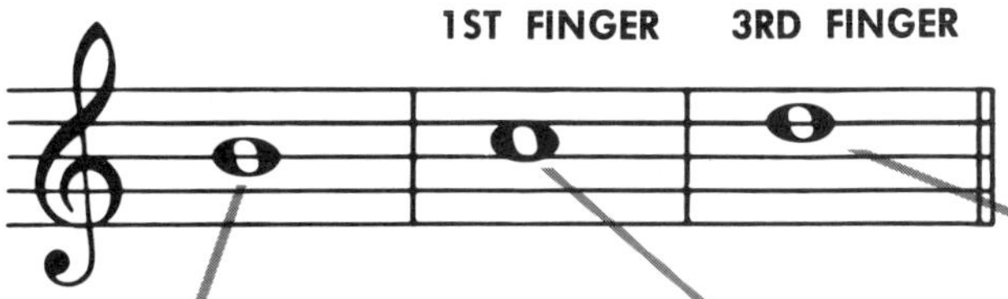

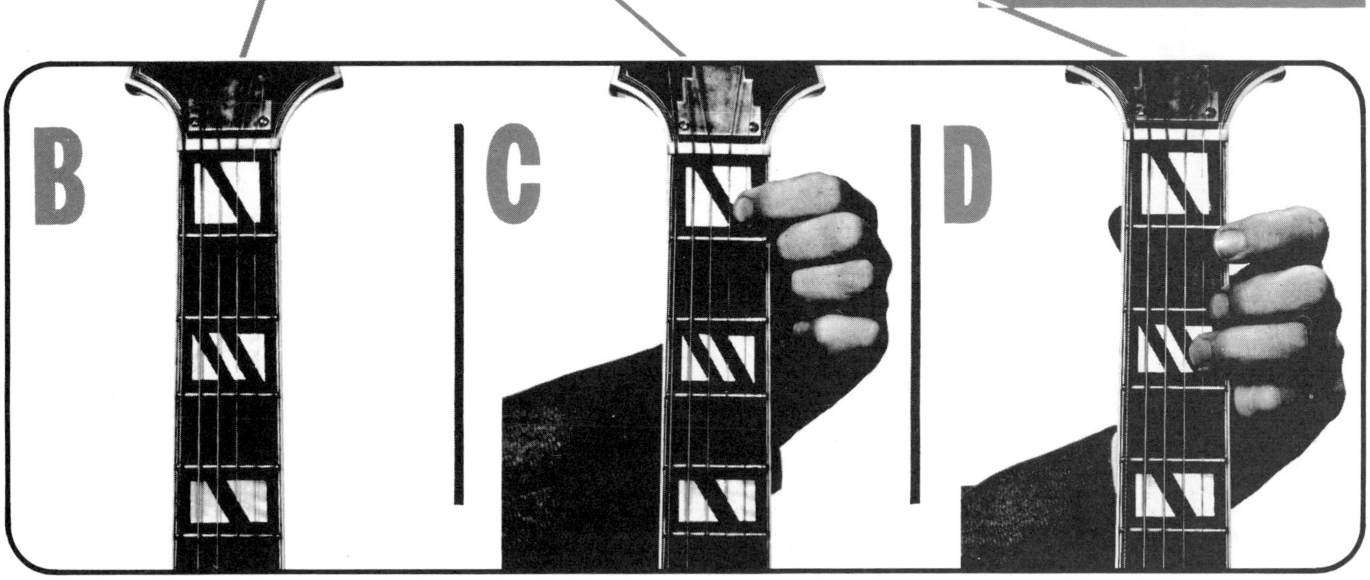

B C D

WHOLE NOTES

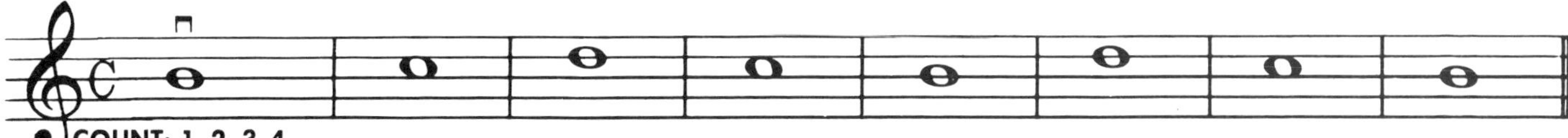

HALF NOTES

QUARTER NOTES

THREE-FOUR TIME

This sign  indicates THREE-FOUR time.

3 — BEATS PER MEASURE.
4 — TYPE OF NOTE RECEIVING ONE BEAT (quarter note).

In THREE-FOUR time, we will have three beats per measure.

DOTTED HALF NOTES

A dot (•) placed behind a note increases its value by one-half.

A dotted half-note (𝅗𝅥.) will receive three beats.

EXAMPLES:

𝅗𝅥 = 2 COUNTS 𝅗𝅥. = 3 COUNTS

The Merry Men

FROLIC

E - B

NOTES ON THE THIRD STRING G

3RD
G
NUT
FRET 1
" 2
A
" 3
" 4

TWO NOTES ON THE 3RD STRING

G (OPEN)

A 2ND FRET 2ND FINGER

G

A

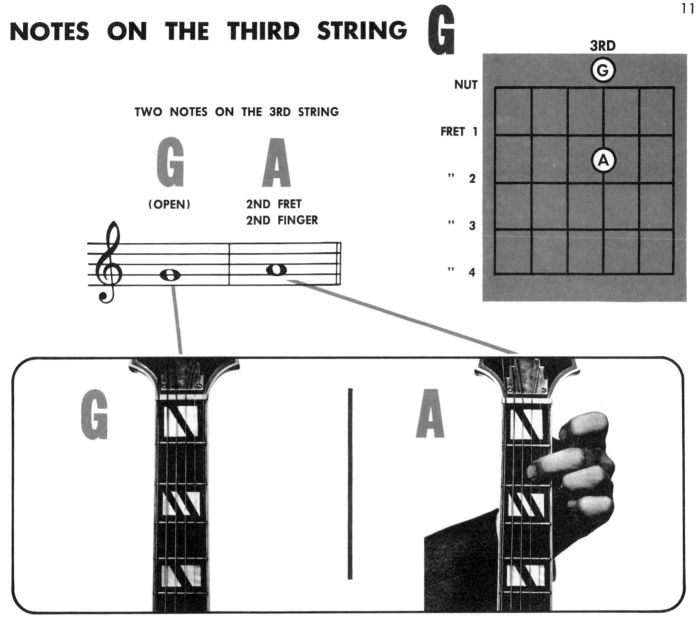

A STUDY ON THE THIRD STRING

Sparkling Stella

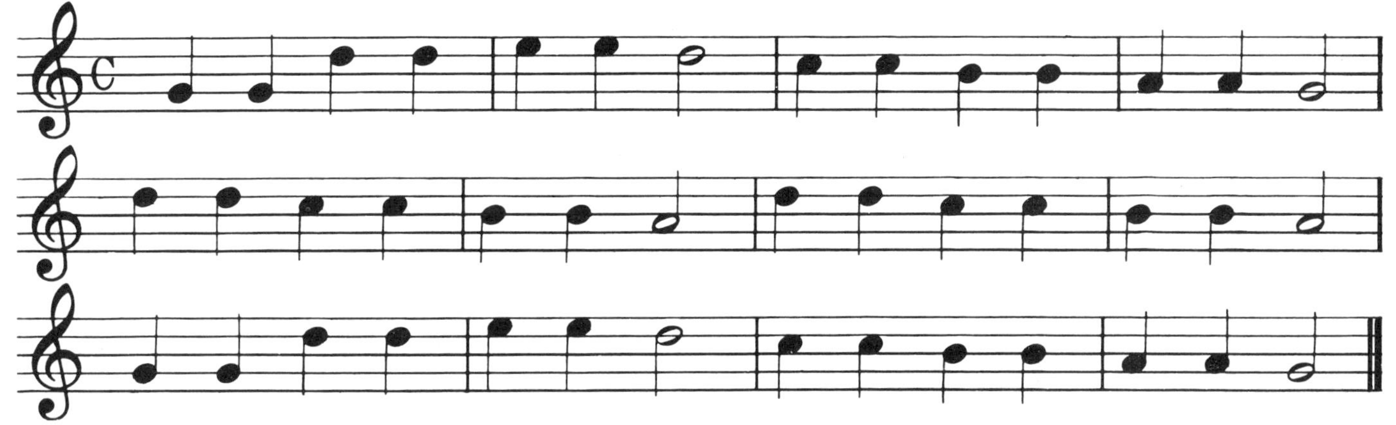

Aura Lee

Teacher Acc:

FOLK SONG

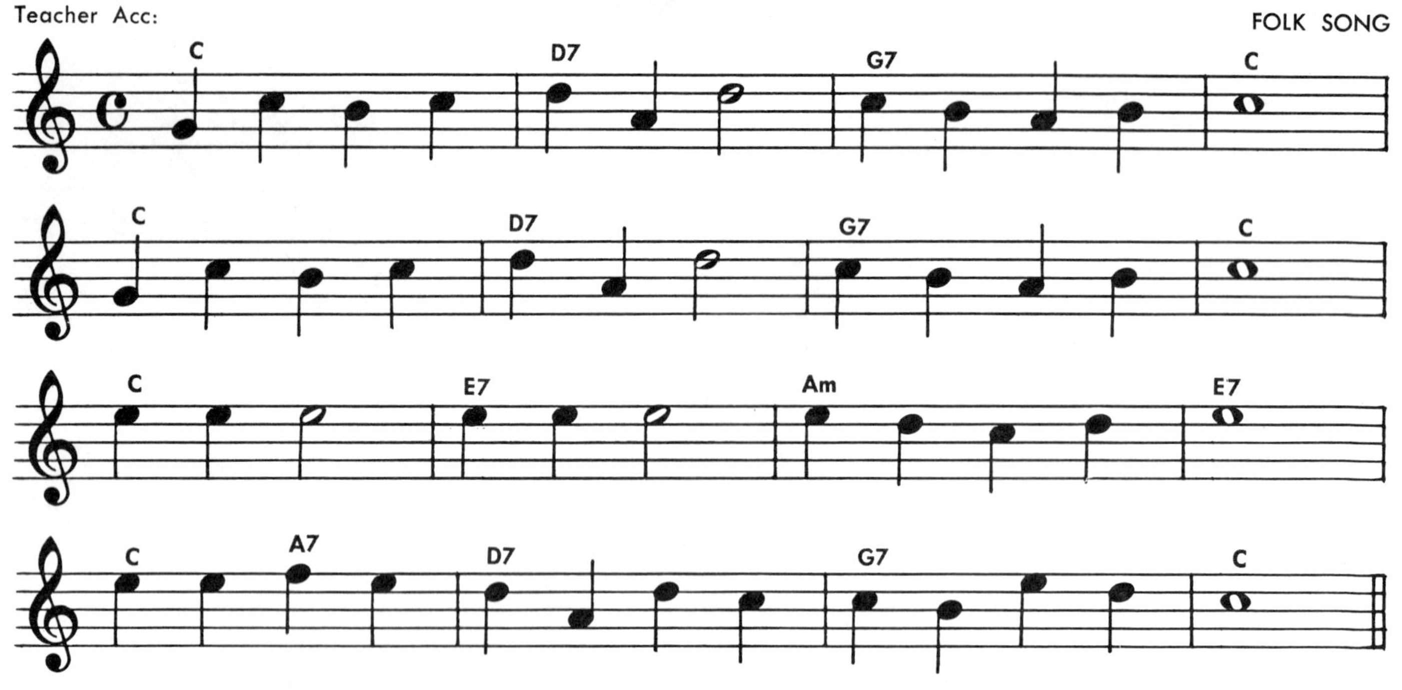

PICK-UP NOTES

One or more notes at the beginning of a strain before the first measure are referred to as pick-up notes.

The rhythm for pick-up notes is taken from the last measure of the selection and the beats are counted as such.

Red River Valley

Teacher Acc:

WESTERN SONG

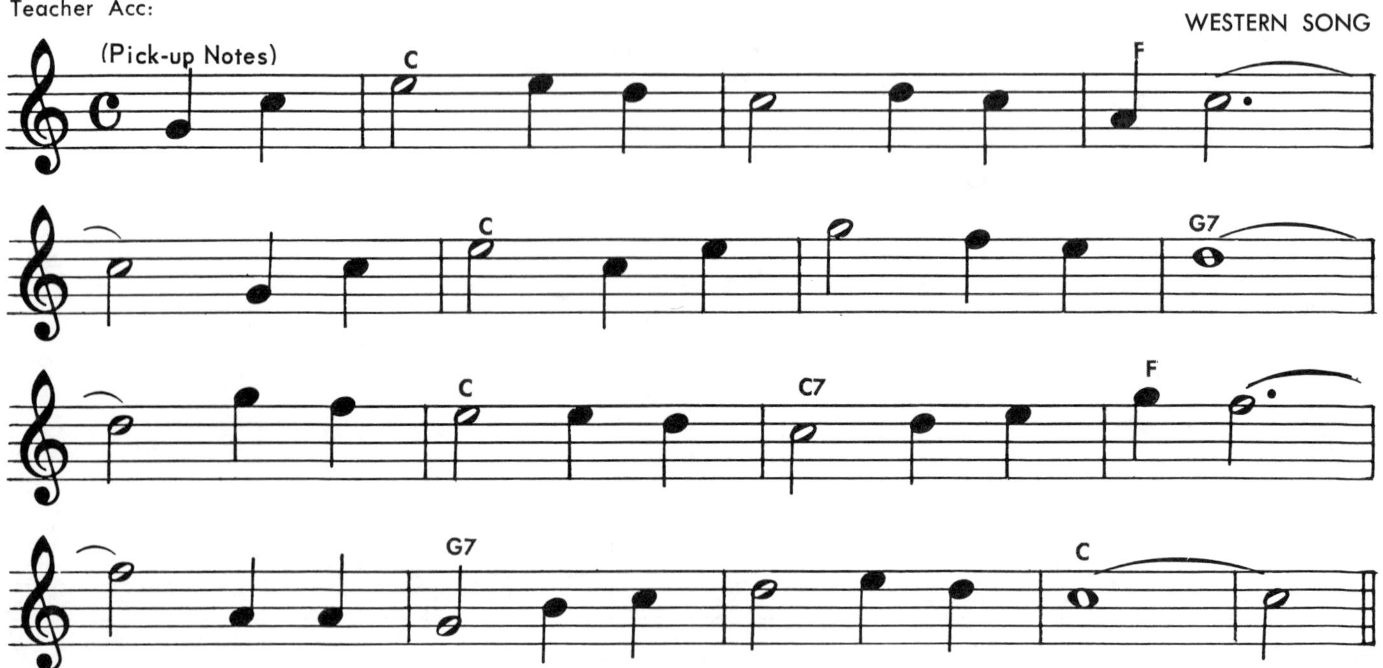

THE TIE

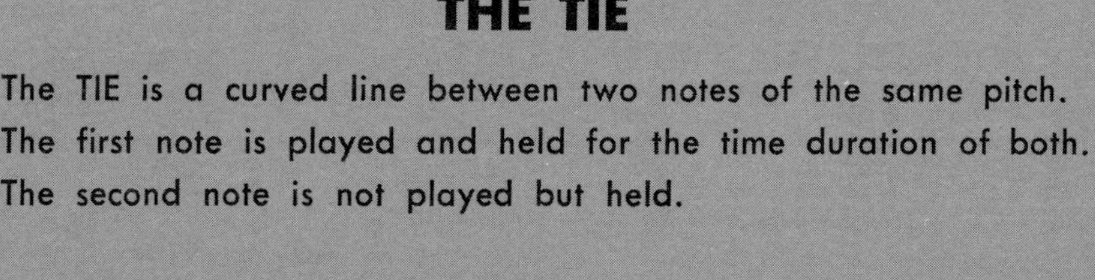
The TIE is a curved line between two notes of the same pitch.
The first note is played and held for the time duration of both.
The second note is not played but held.

Psalm 100

When The Saints Go Marchin' In

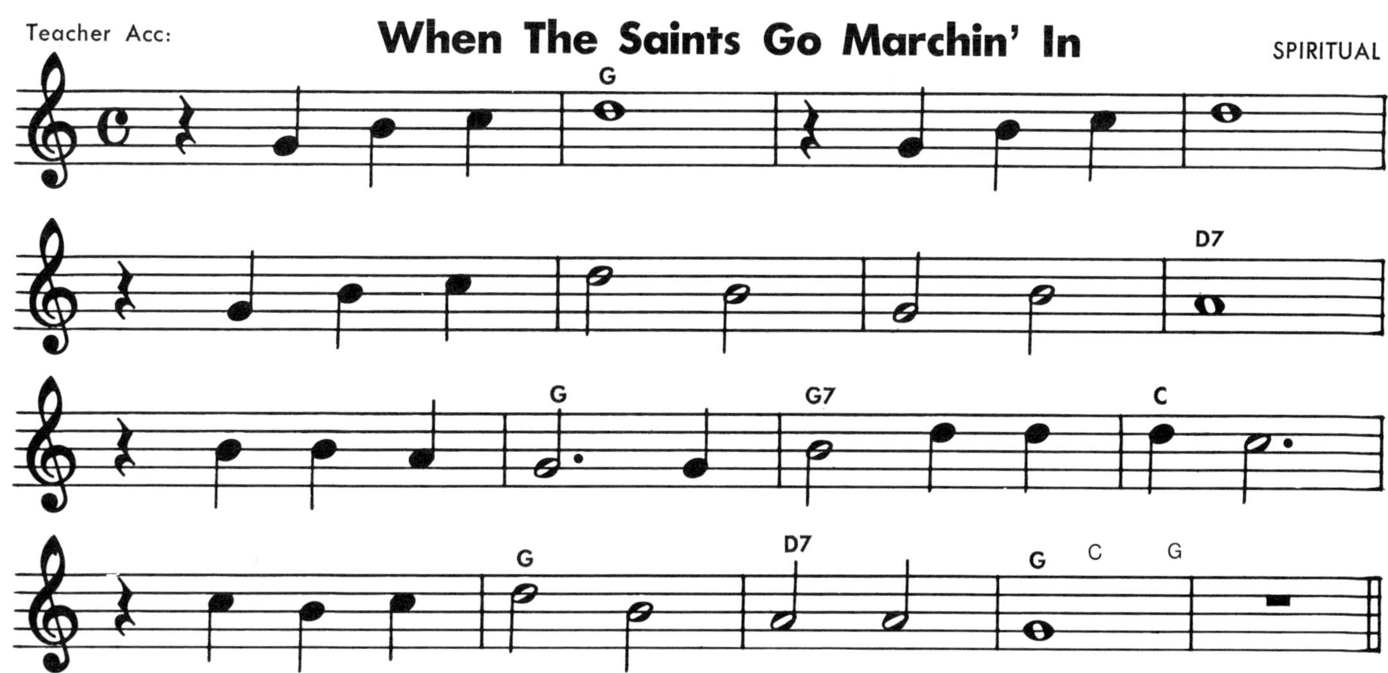

NOTES ON THE FOURTH STRING D

THREE NOTES ON THE 4TH STRING

D E F

(OPEN) — 2ND FRET 2ND FINGER — 3RD FRET 3RD FINGER

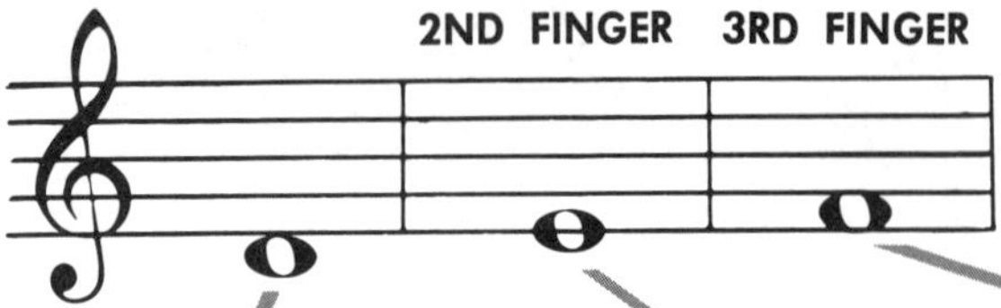

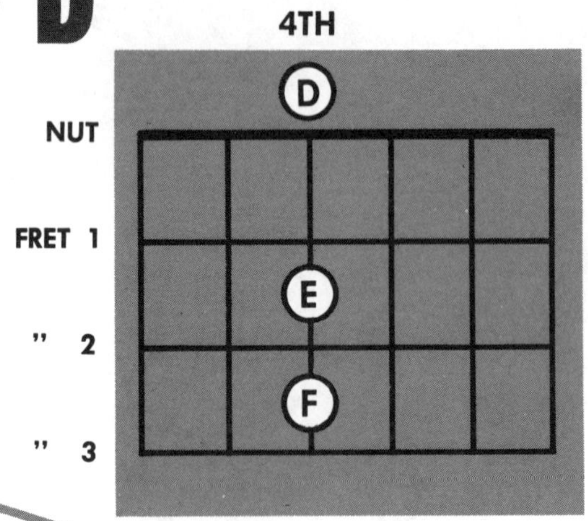

WHOLE NOTES

HALF NOTES

QUARTER NOTES

THE EIGHTH NOTE

An eighth note receives one-half beat. (One quarter note equals two eighth notes).

An eighth note will have a head, stem, and flag. If two or more are in successive order they may be connected by a bar. (See Example).

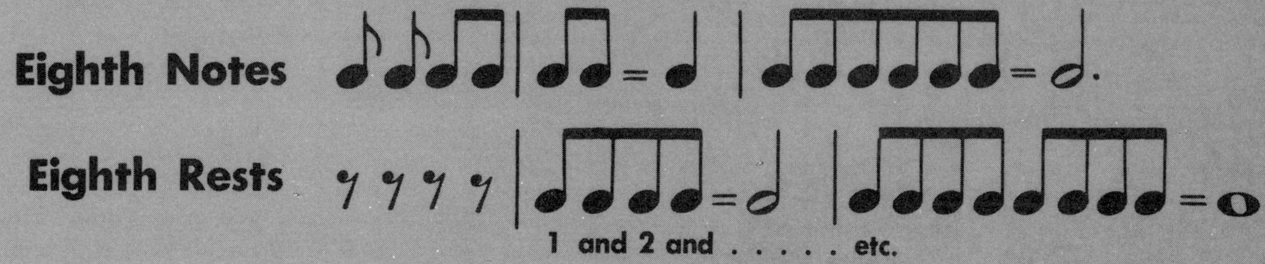

Eighth Note Studies

(⊓ V Down-up)

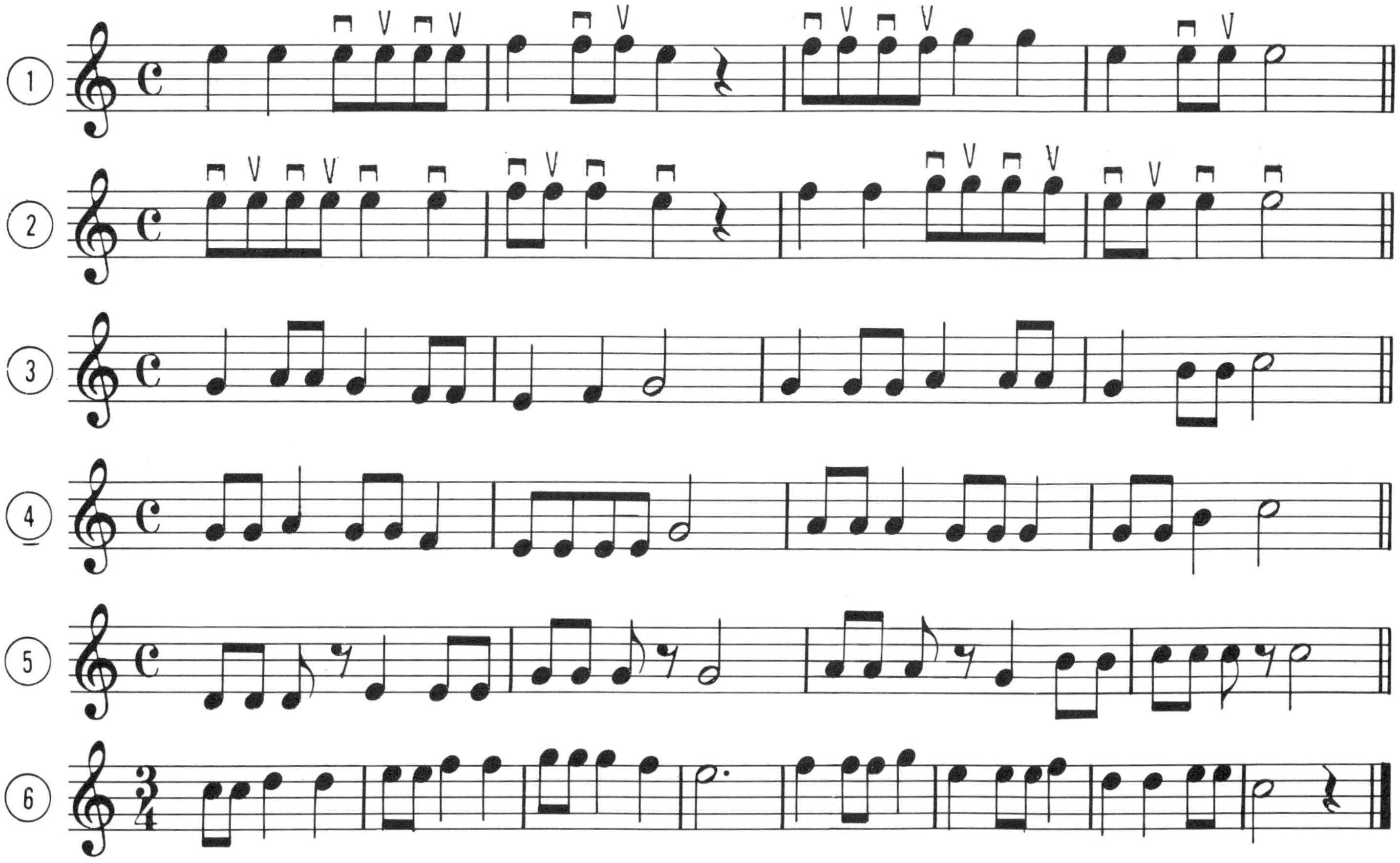

1

2

3

4

5

6

Amazing Grace

Teacher Acc:

HYMN

Tenting Tonight

SONG OF THE CIVIL WAR

Teacher Acc:

Melancholy

Teacher Acc:

LEDGER LINES:

When the pitch of a musical sound is below or above the staff, the notes are then placed on, or between, extra lines called LEDGER LINES.

THEY WILL BE LIKE THIS:

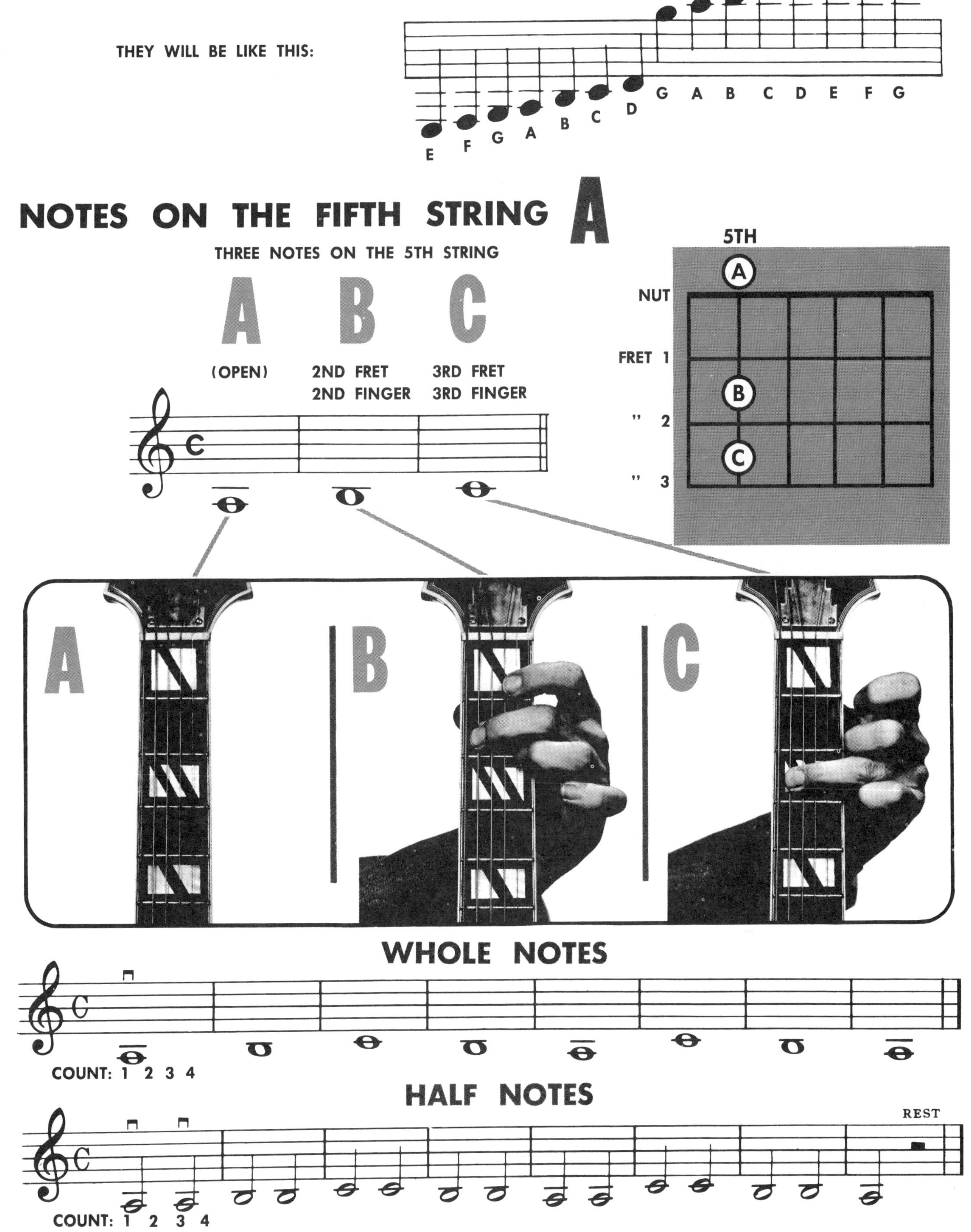

QUARTER NOTES

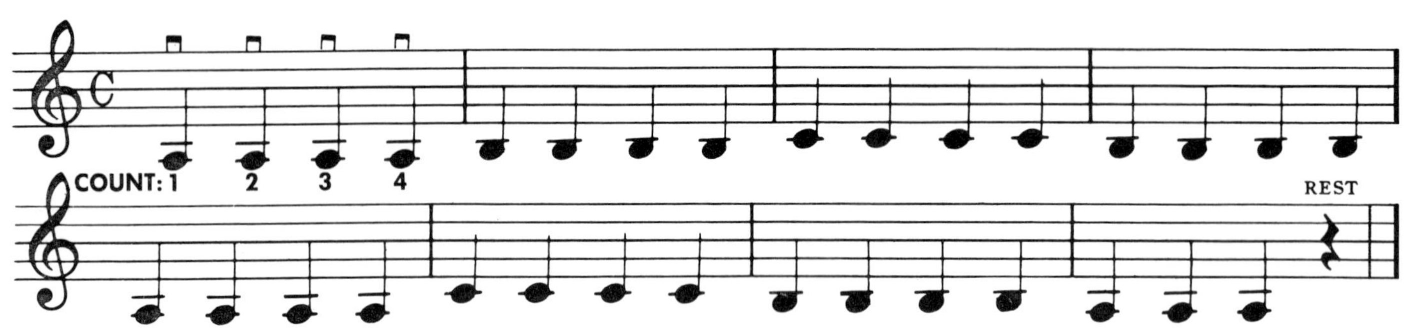

Buffalo Gals

WESTERN SONG

C G7 C

G7 C

G7 C

G7 C

Chester

Teacher Acc:

SONG OF THE REVOLUTIONARY WAR

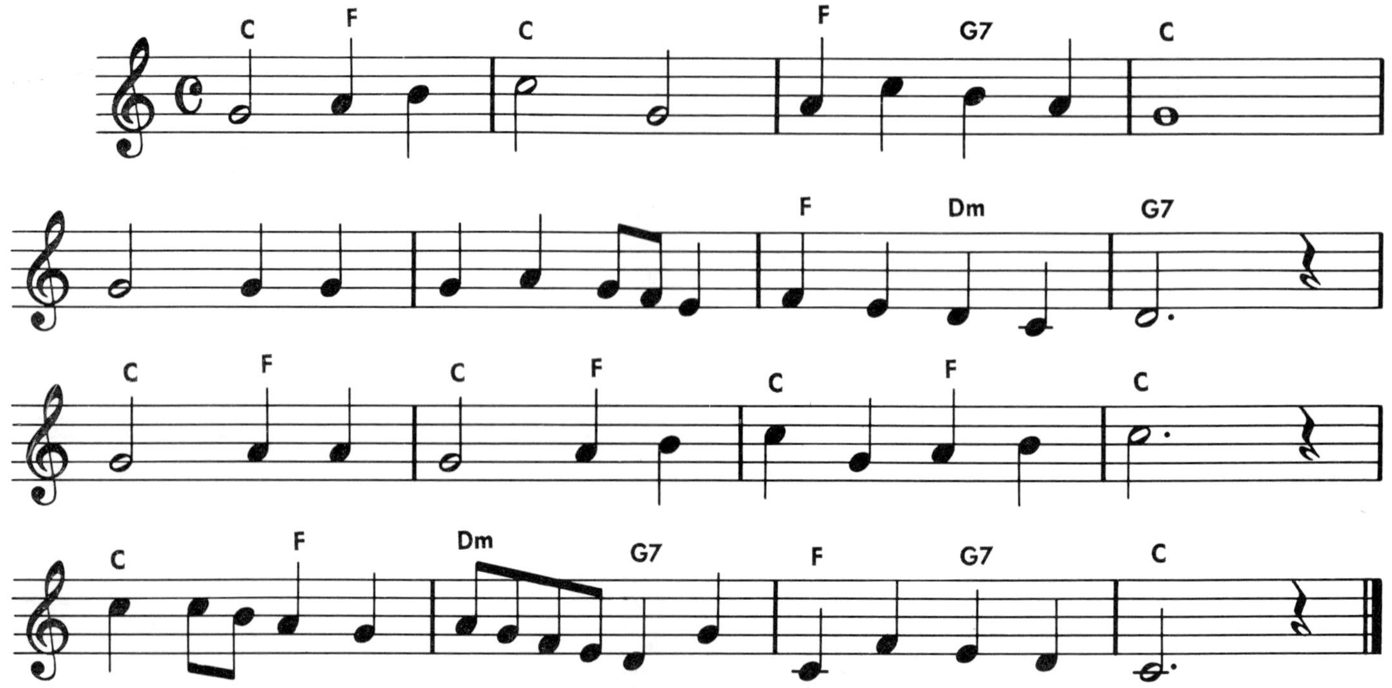

C F C F G7 C

F Dm G7

C F C F C F C

C F Dm G7 F G7 C

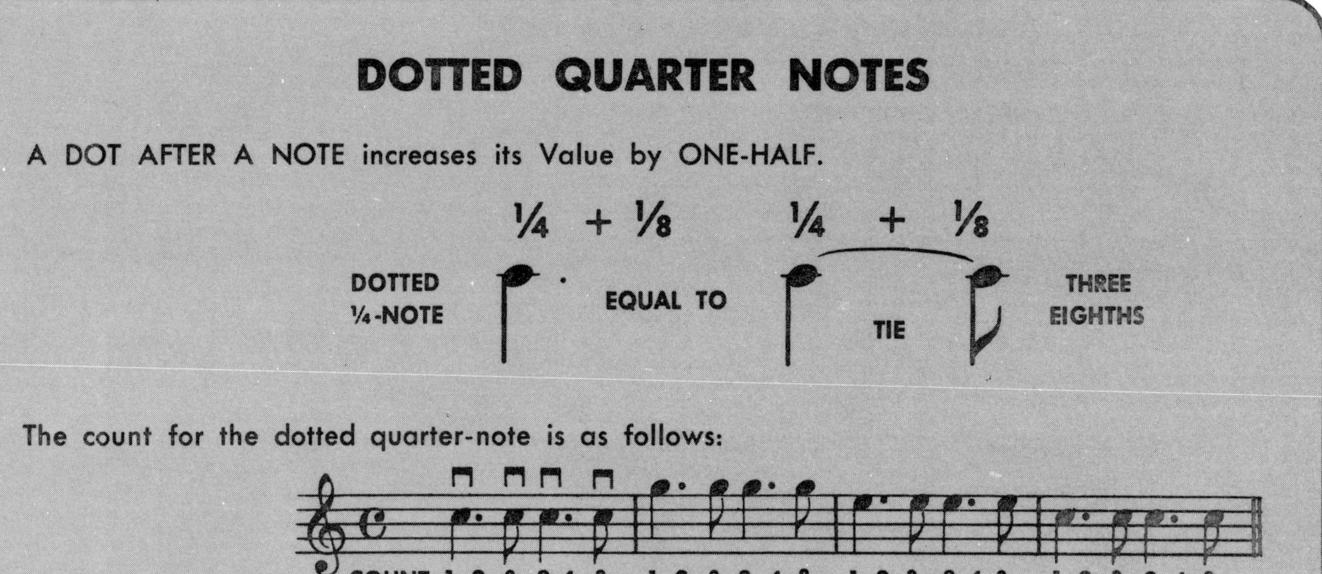

Kum-Ba-Ya

AFRICAN HYMN

Michael, Row The Boat Ashore

SPIRITUAL

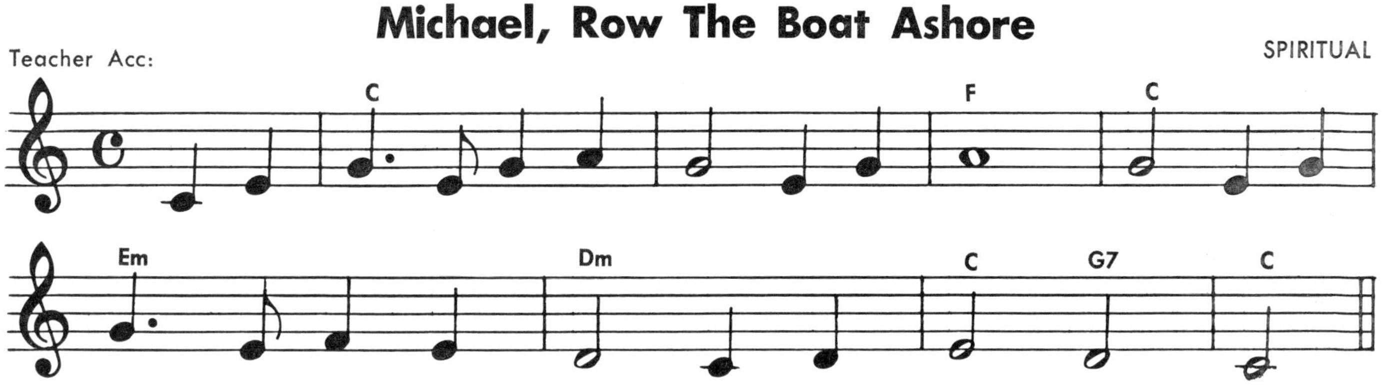

NOTES ON THE SIXTH STRING E

THREE NOTES ON THE 6TH STRING

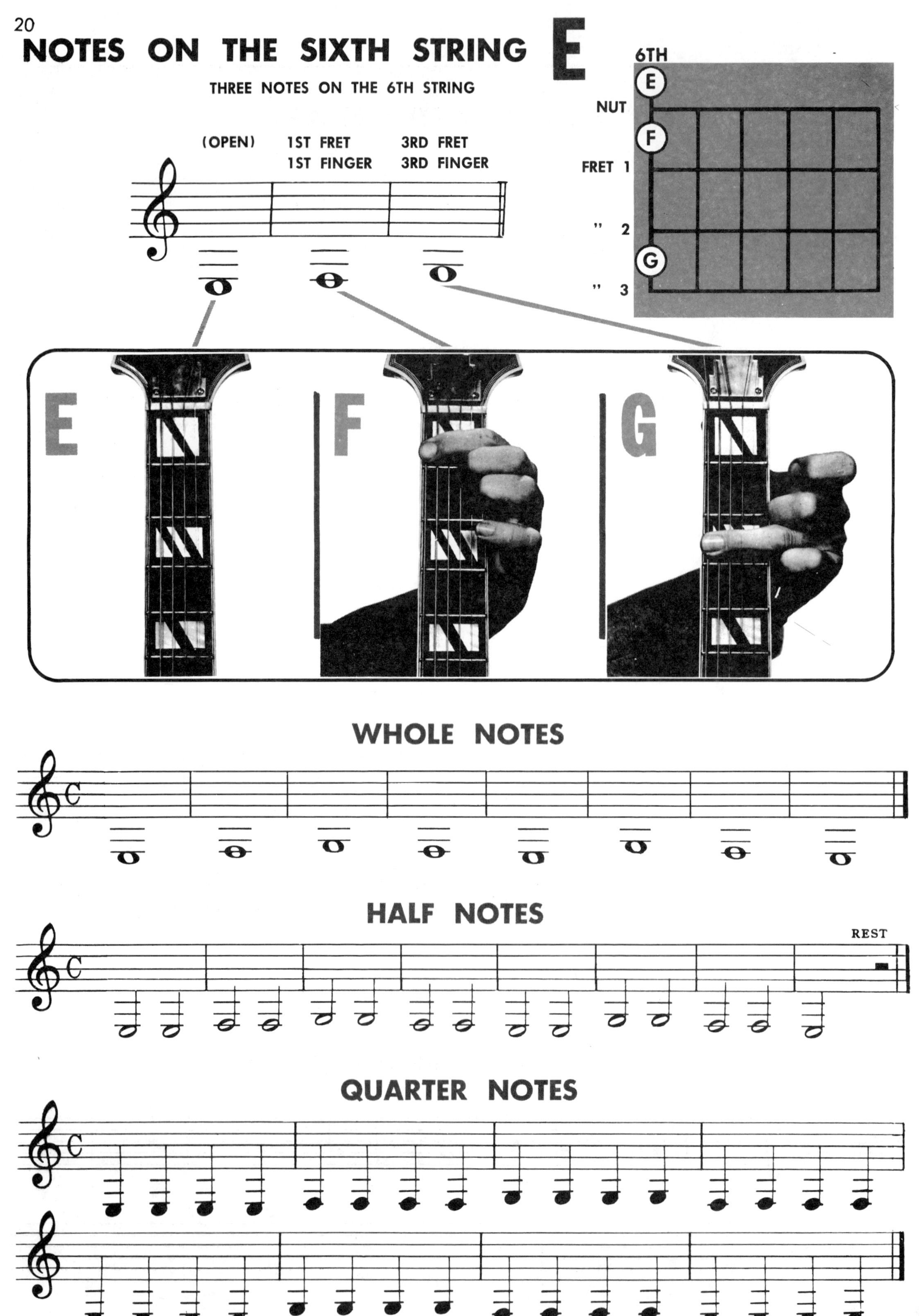

INTRODUCING THE A NOTE

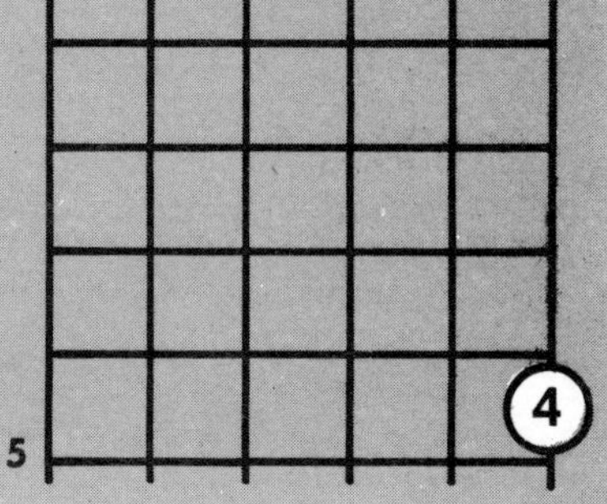

MINOR MELODY

THE NOTES ON THE GUITAR IN THE FIRST POSITION

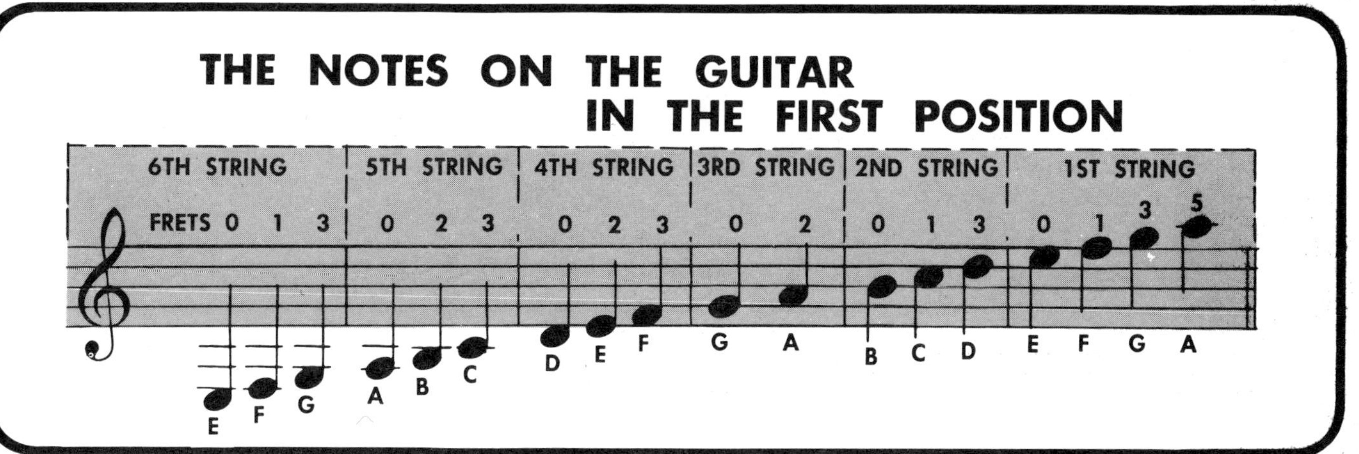

Hitting On All Six

MEL BAY

A WORD ABOUT DUETS

One of the first requisites of a good guitarist is the ability to play well with others. It is with this point in mind that I am stressing the value of duet training.

The Modern Guitarist has to have the ability to play SOLO, HARMONY and RHYTHM.

Duet training will teach the student to perform his own part independently without the bewilderment or confusion caused by the rhythm or counterpoint appearing in the second part.

This is one of the most important phases of the student's training.

The second part in the following duets will be played by the teacher. The student will be required to play both parts later.

Our First Duet

GUITAR DUET

Arr. by Mel Bay

STUDENT

Count: 1 2 3 4

TEACHER

STUDENT

TEACHER

DOTS BEFORE AND AFTER A DOUBLE BAR MEAN REPEAT THE MEASURES BETWEEN.

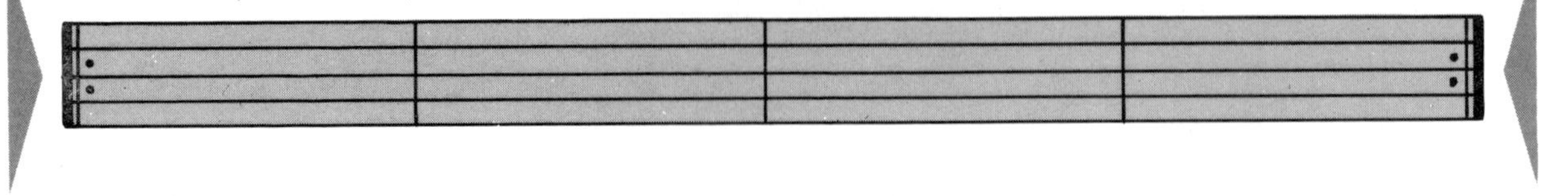

The Repeater

I = 1st part.
II = 2nd part.

The dots placed above and below the third line of the staff at the double-bar indicate that the piece is to be repeated.

CHORDS

A MELODY is a succession of single tones.

A CHORD is a combination of tones sounded together.

TONES IN A MELODY.

THE SAME TONES AS A CHORD.

We will construct our chords by playing the chordal tones separately as in a melody and **without raising the fingers**, striking them together.

The Chord Waltz

MEL BAY

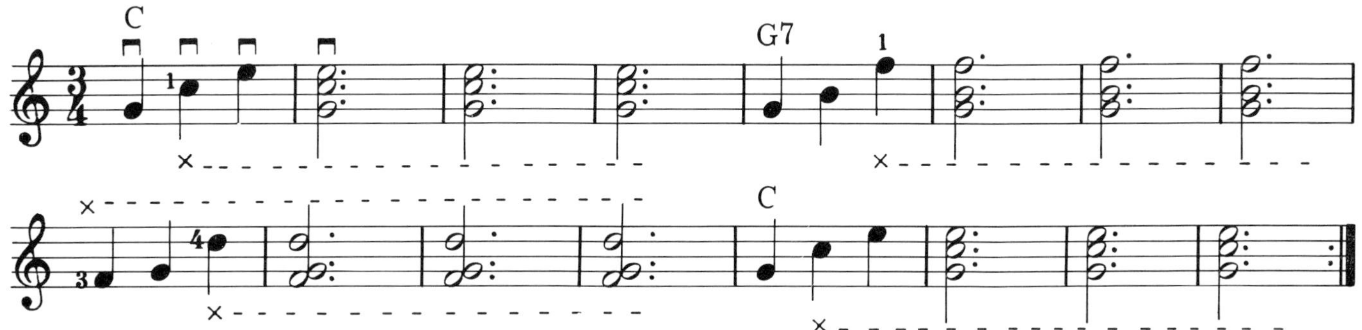

The Builder

MEL BAY

Small Chord Etude

MEL BAY

Practice the above etude until it can be played without missing a beat.

*Note that the first finger holds down two notes (C-F) in the second chord.

FOUR-STRING CHORD STUDY

We use the same method for building four-string chords as we did in building the three-string chords. Play the chordal tones melodically holding the fingers down until chord is reached then strike them together producing the desired chord.

Exercise

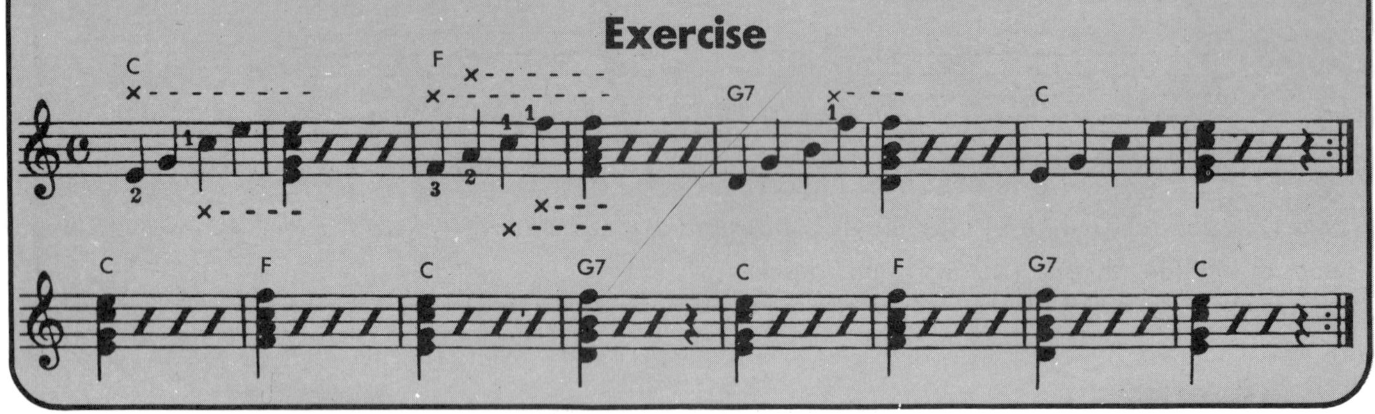

GUITAR DUET

Follow The Leader

Arr. by Mel Bay

I

Count: 2 3 4 1 2 3 4

II

BASS SOLOS WITH CHORD ACCOMPANIMENT

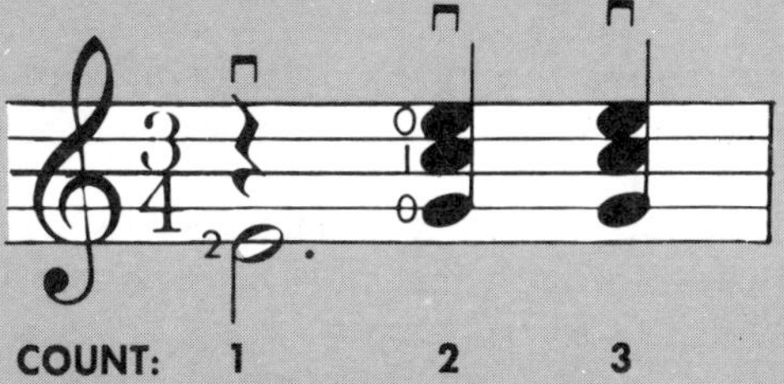

When playing bass solos with chord accompaniment you will find the solo with the stems turned **downward** and the accompaniment with the stems turned **upward.**

In the example shown above you see the dotted half-note (E) with the stem downward. It is played on the count of **one** and is **held** for counts **two** and **three.**

The quarter rest over the dotted half-note indicates that there is **no chord accompaniment at the count of one.** The chords with the stems upward are played on counts of **two** and **three.**

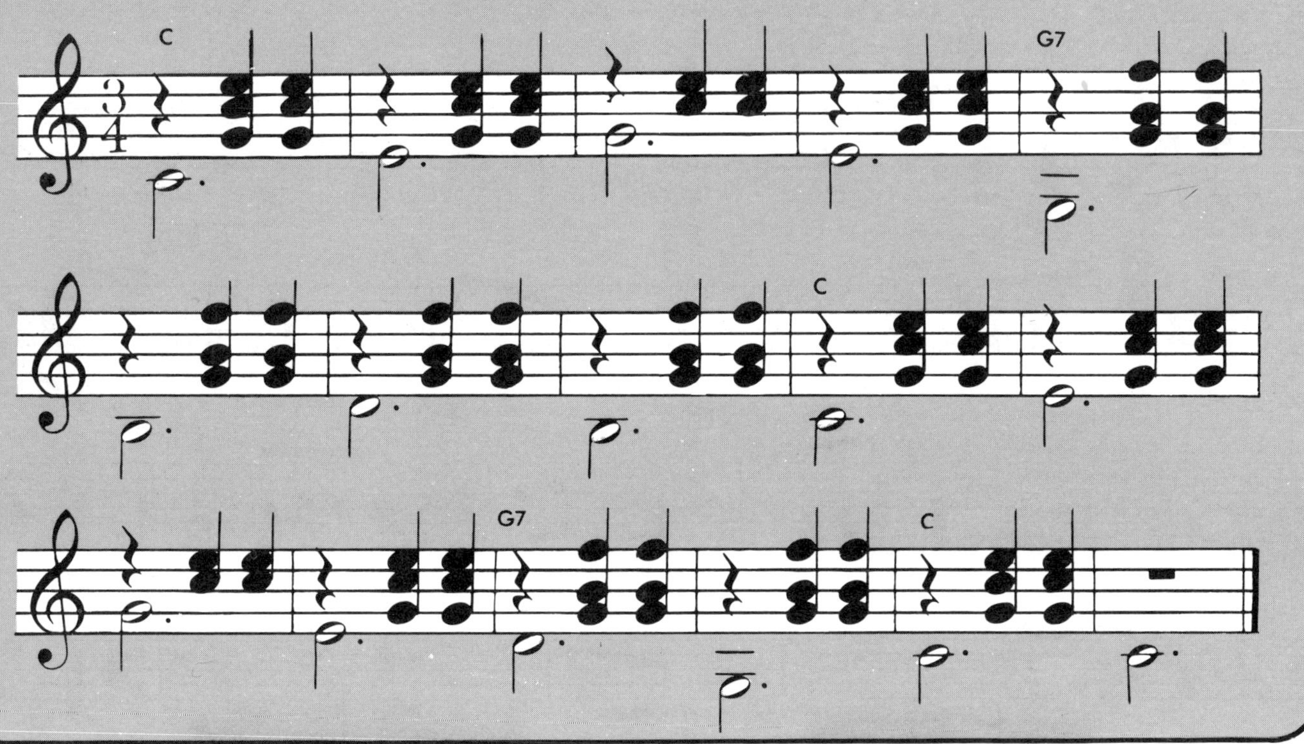

Gliding Along

THE KEY OF C All music studied so far in this book has been in the Key of C.

That means that the notes have been taken from the C Scale (shown at right) and made into melodies.

It is called the C Scale because the first note is C and we proceed through the musical alphabet until C reappears. C-D-E-F-G-A-B-C.

We will cover the subject of keys and scales more thoroughly in the Theory and Harmony Chapters appearing later on in this course.

At present we will deal only with basic fundamentals.

THE C SCALE

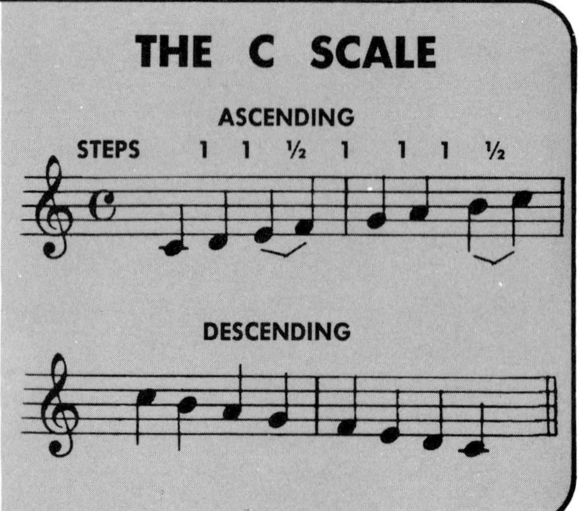

SHENANDOAH

The Blue Bells Of Scotland

GUITAR SOLO

Arr. by Mel Bay

CHORDS IN THE KEY OF C MAJOR

The key of C has three principal chords. They are C, F, and G7.

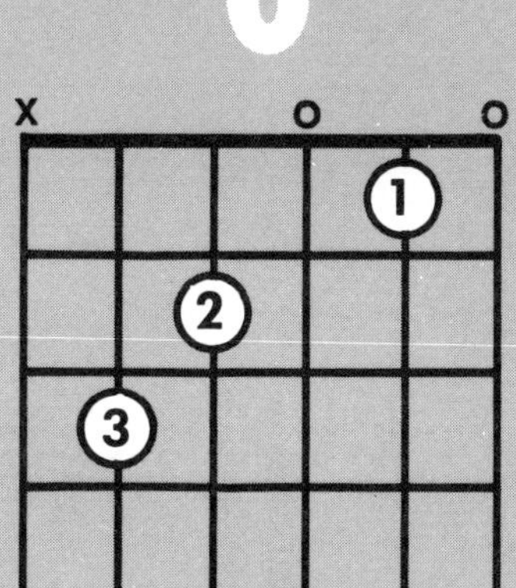

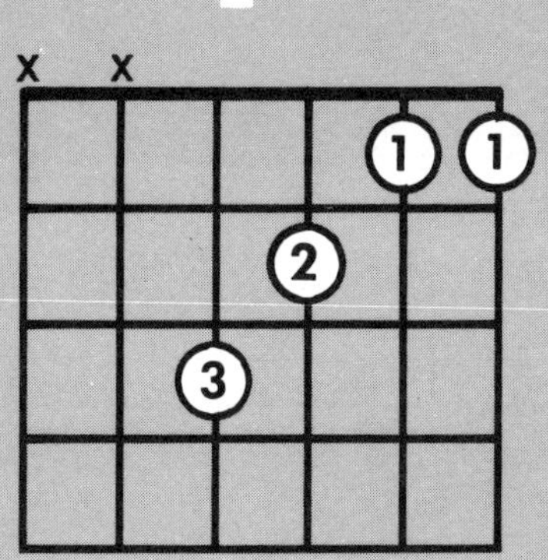

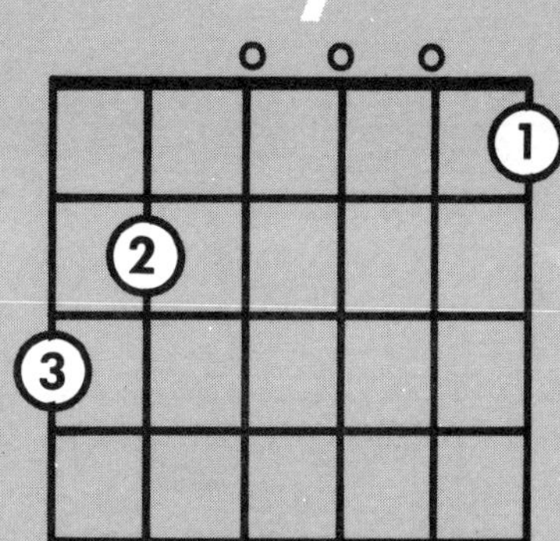

The circles indicate the positions to place your fingers.

Numerals inside circles indicate the fingers.

(x) over the strings means that the strings are **not** to be played.

(o) over the strings indicates the strings to be played open.

Place fingers on positions indicated by the circles and strike them all together.

Musical Notation Of The Chords

In Three-Four Time

 GUITAR SOLO

Long, Long Ago

Arr. by Mel Bay

Andante

STEPS

A Half-Step is the distance from a given tone to the next higher or lower tone. On the Guitar the distance of a Half-Step is ONE FRET.

A Whole-Step consists of TWO Half-Steps.

The distance of a Whole-Step on the Guitar is TWO FRETS.

The C Scale has two half-steps. They are between E-F and B-C.

Note the distance of one fret between those notes. The distances between C-D, D-E, F-G, G-A, and A-B are Whole-Steps.

Whole-Steps and Half-Steps are also referred to as Whole-Tones and Half-Tones. We will refer to them as Whole-Steps and Half-Steps.

A Daily Scale Study

MEL BAY

The above study should be played slowly with a gradual increase of speed until a moderate tempo has been reached. It is an excellent daily exercise.

CHROMATICS

The alteration of the pitches of tones is brought about by the use of symbols called CHROMATICS. (Also referred to as ACCIDENTALS)

The Sharp ♯

THE SHARP PLACED BEFORE A NOTE RAISES ITS PITCH ½-STEP OR ONE FRET.

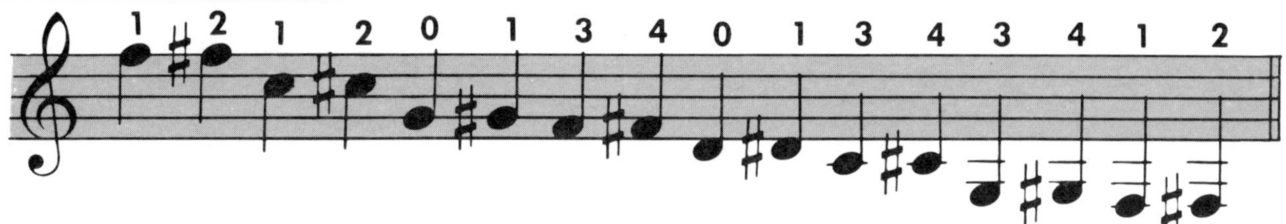

The Flat ♭

THE FLAT PLACED BEFORE A NOTE LOWERS ITS PITCH ½-STEP OR ONE FRET.

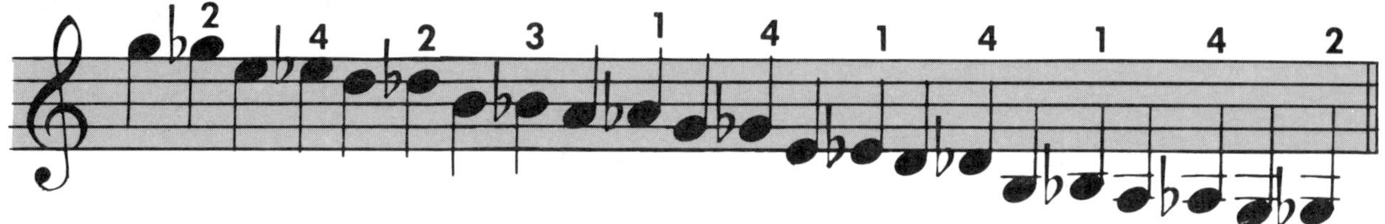

The Natural ♮

THE NATURAL RESTORES A NOTE TO ITS NORMAL POSITION. IT CANCELS ALL ACCIDENTALS PREVIOUSLY USED.

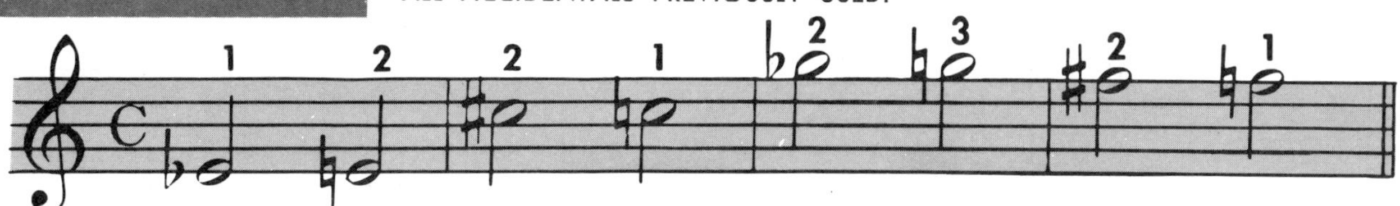

Running Around

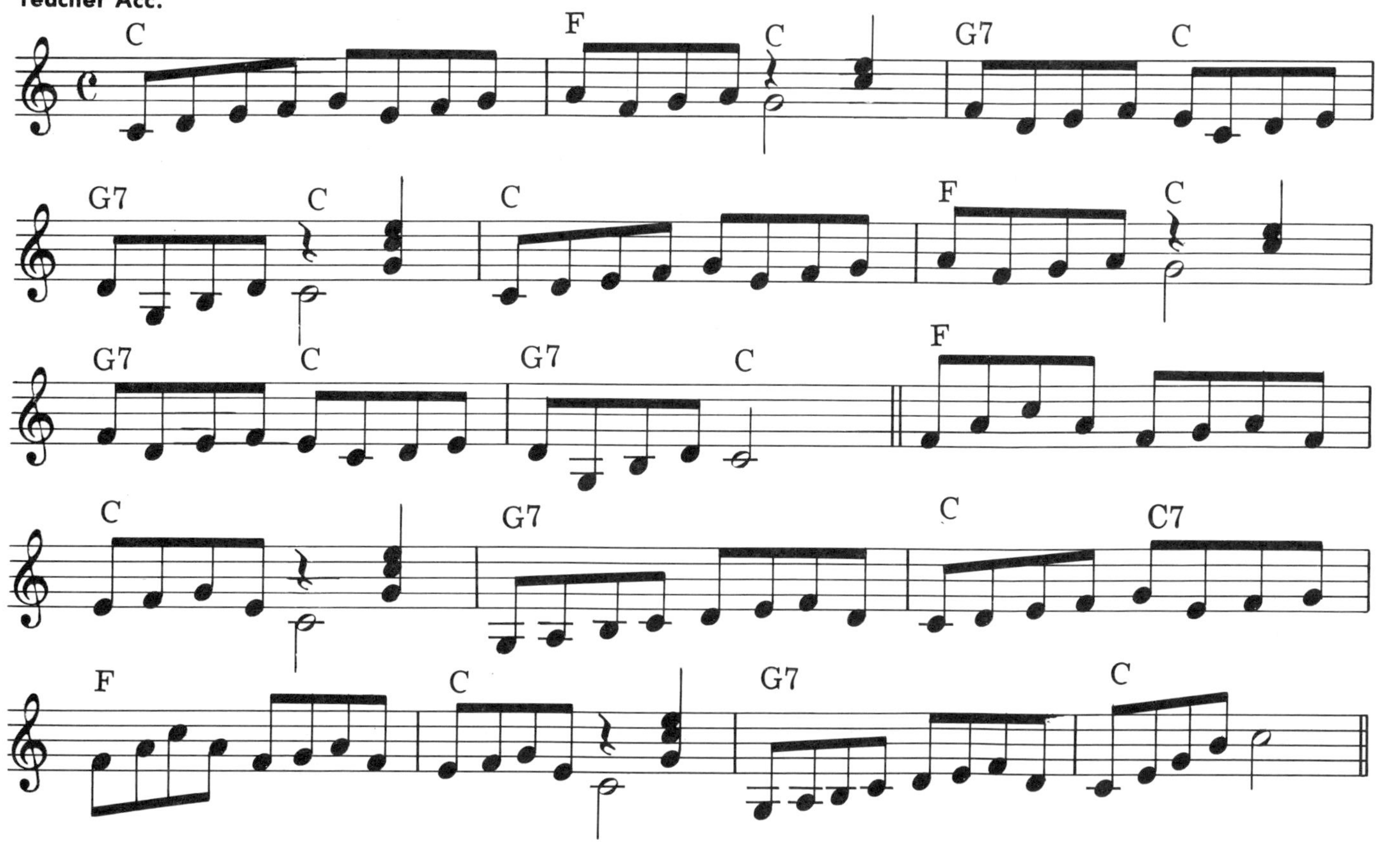

 GUITAR SOLO

Home, Home, Can I Forget Thee

Arr. by Mel Bay

TEMPO

Tempo is the rate of speed of a musical composition. Three types of tempo used in this book will be:

ANDANTE: A slow easy pace.
MODERATO: Moderate.
ALLEGRO: Lively.

GUITAR DUET

Playtime

PLEYEL
Arr. by Mel Bay

Moderato

I
Count:3 1 2 3
II

I
II

I
II

I
II

THE KEY OF A MINOR

(Relative to C Major)

Each Major key will have a Relative Minor key.

The Relative Minor Scale is built upon the **sixth tone** of the Major Scale.

The Key Signature of both will be the same.

The Minor Scale will have the same number of tones (7) as the Major.

The difference between the two scales is the arrangement of the whole-steps and half-steps.

There are **three forms** of the minor scale: 1. PURE or NATURAL, 2. HARMONIC, 3. MELODIC.

The A Minor Scale

Natural (Pure)

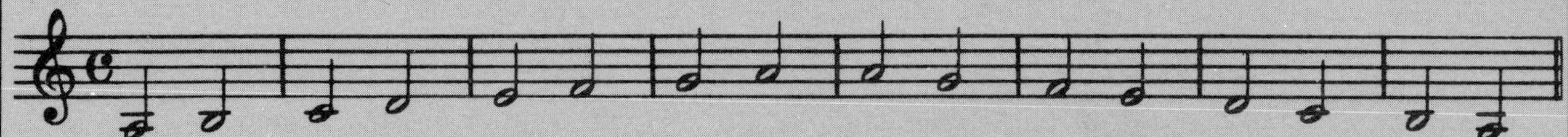

Harmonic

The 7th tone is raised one half-step ascending and descending.

Melodic

The 6th and 7th tones are raised one half-step ascending and lowered back to their normal pitch descending.

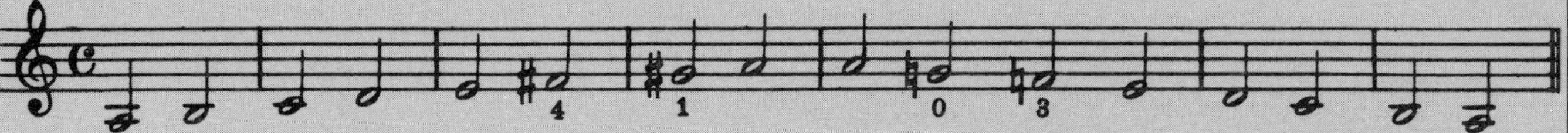

The Chords In The Key Of A Minor

M = Minor

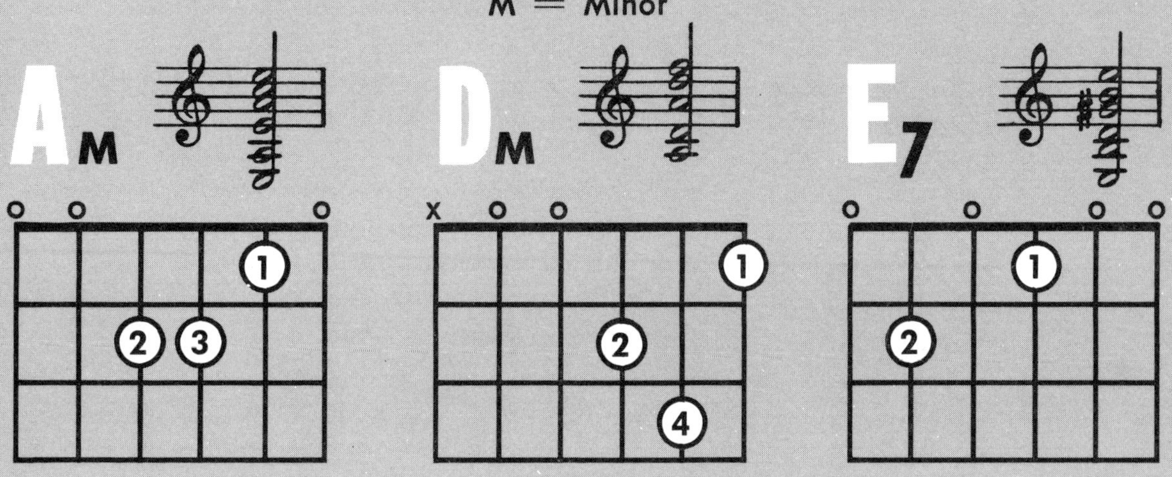

Accompaniment Styles In A Minor

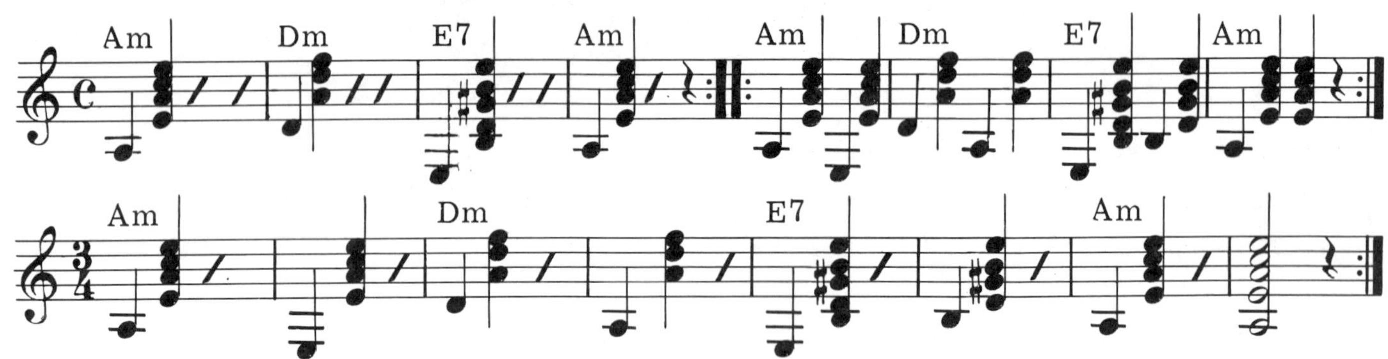

Orchestration Style

The diagonal line (/) indicates a chord-stroke. They will fall only on each beat of the measure.

In the above exercise no bass is used . . . only the chords.
Repeat the accompaniment exercises until they can be played without missing a beat.

A Daily Scale Study In A Minor

Hold Sign: 𝄐 This sign placed over or under a note or rest, indicates the prolonging of its time value.

WAYFARIN' STRANGER

FIRST AND SECOND ENDINGS

Sometimes two endings are required in certain selections . . . one to lead back into a repeated chorus and one to close it.

They will be shown like this:

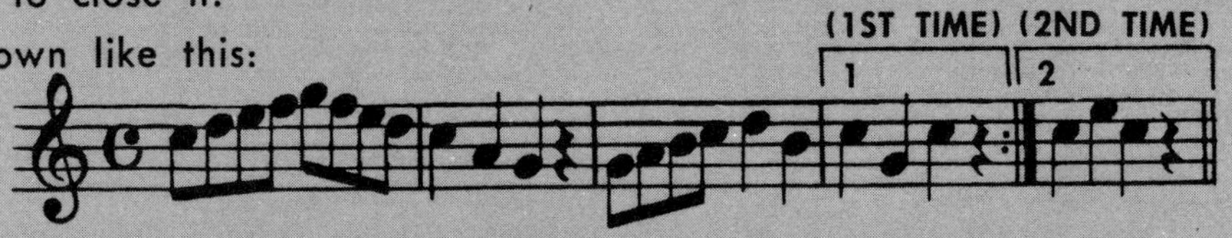

(1ST TIME) (2ND TIME)

1 2

The first time play the bracketed ending **No. 1.** Repeat the chorus.
The second time skip the first ending and play ending **No. 2.**

WORDS INDICATING VARIATIONS OF TEMPO

RITARDANDO or RITARD . . . (rit.) . . . To grow slower

ACCELERANDO . . . (acc.) . . . To increase the speed or tempo

I

II

Fine

1.

2.

D.C. al Fine

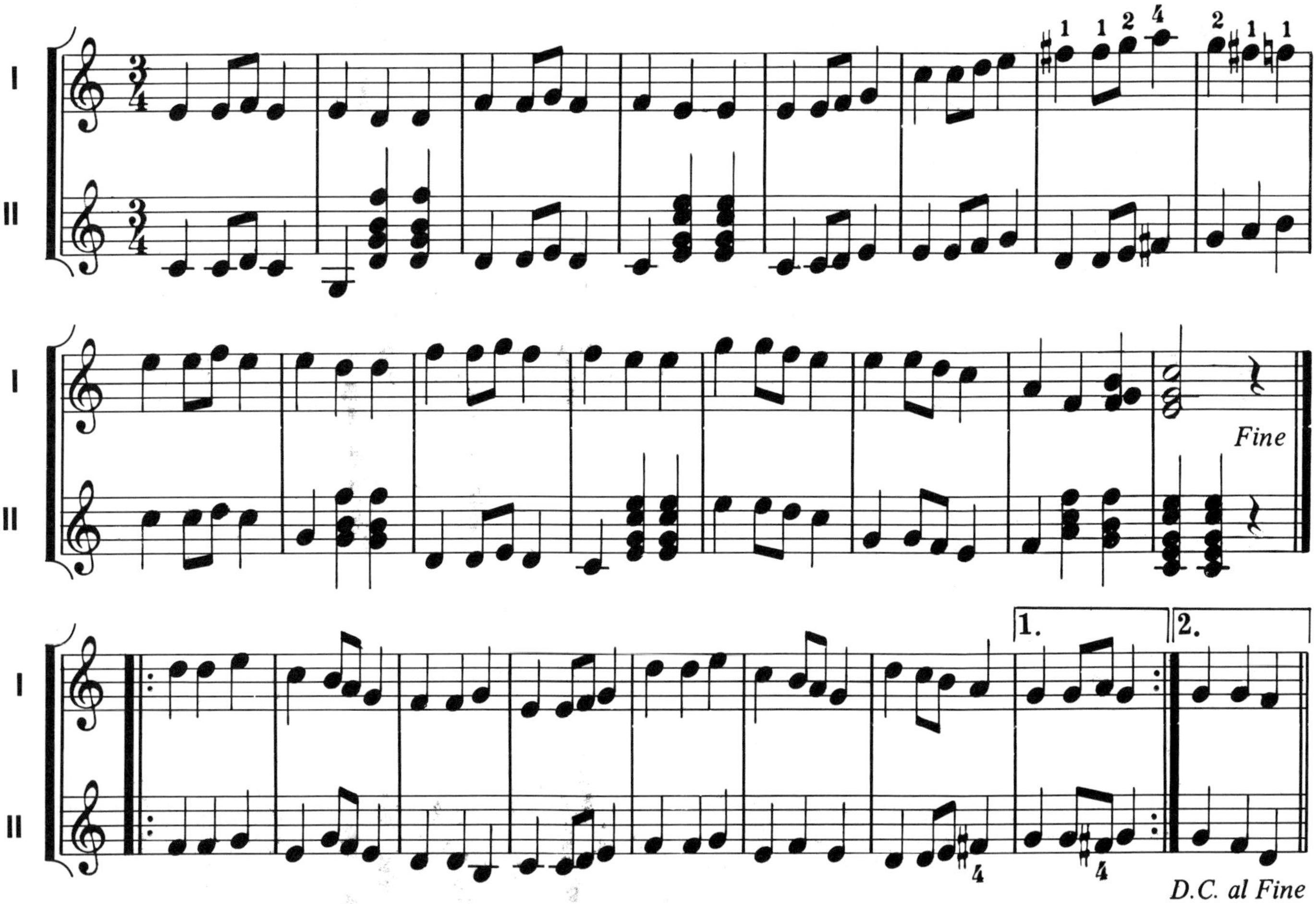

*D.C. al Fine . . . Repeat from the begining to the word Fine.

Another Daily Scale Study In A Minor

Melodic

THE UP STROKE

V = **UP STROKE.** This stroke will be used on repeated eighth-notes of the same pitch.

A Visit To The Relatives

Careless Love

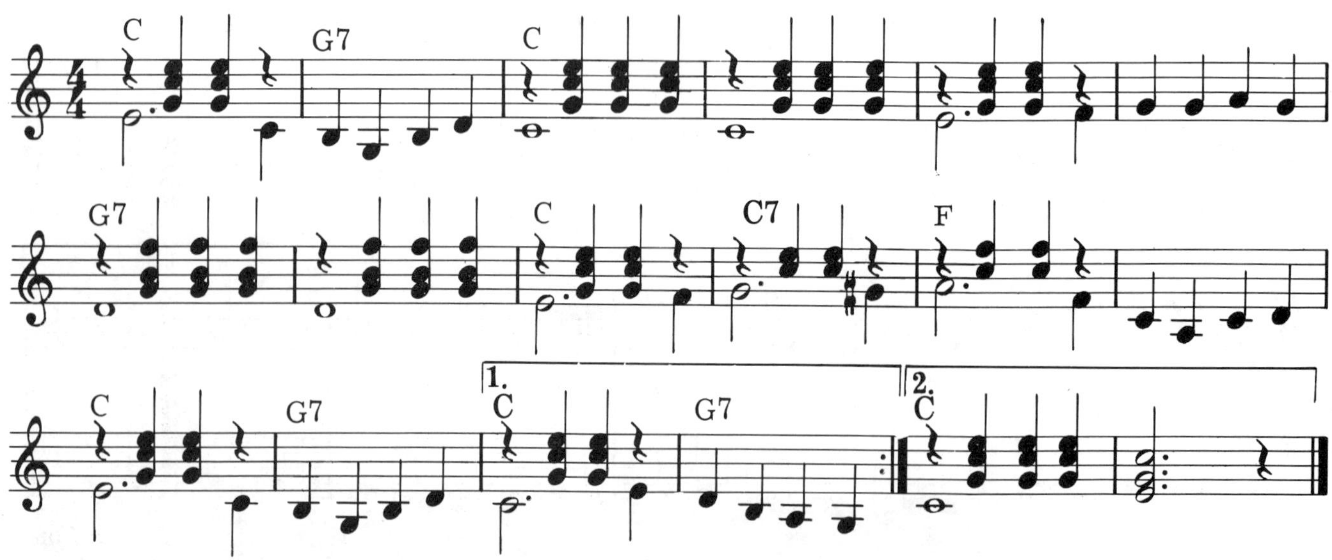

Song Without Words

GUITAR DUET

Arr. by Mel Bay

I
II
Fine
D.C. al Fine

Terry's Tune

C
Dm
G7
Hold
Fine
D.C. al Fine

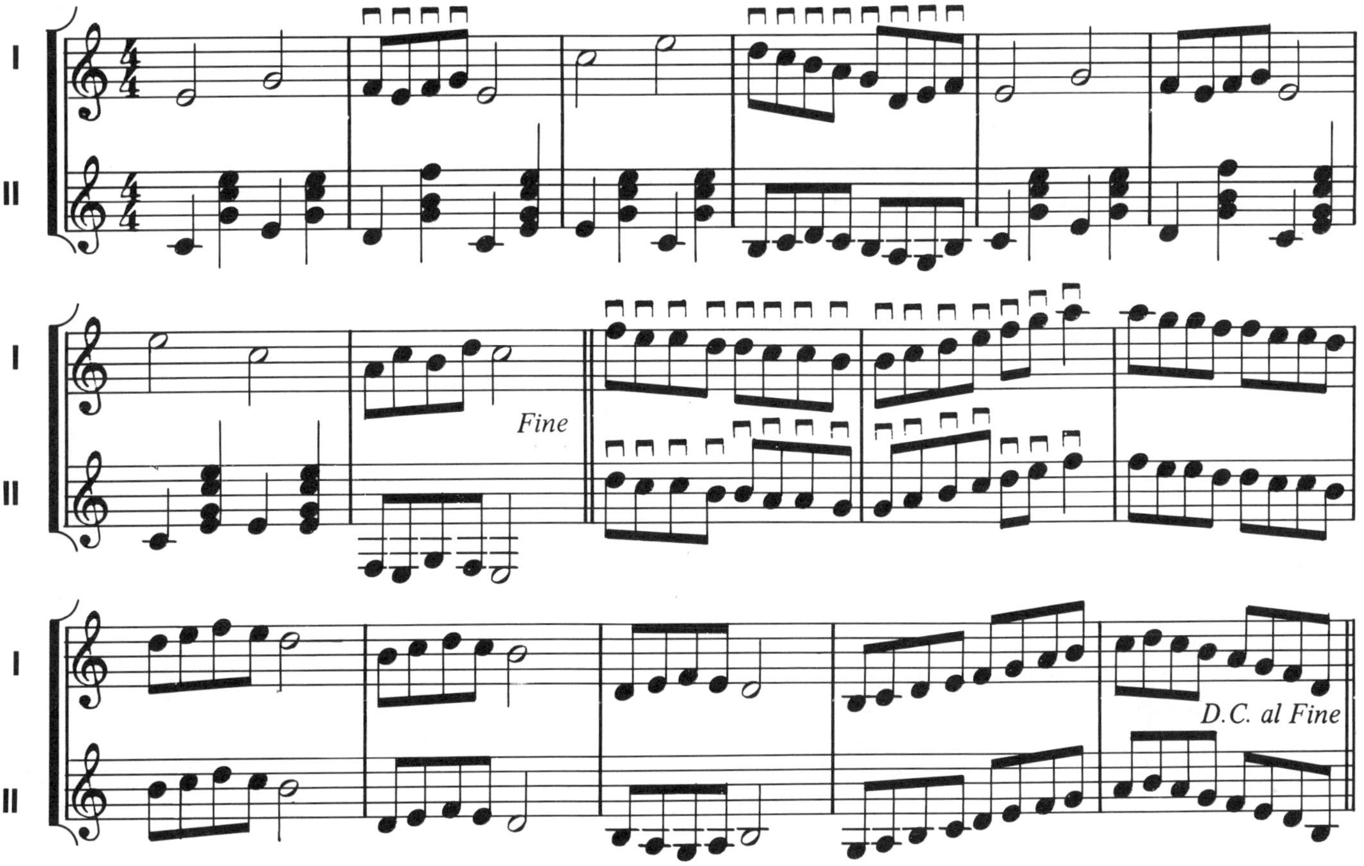

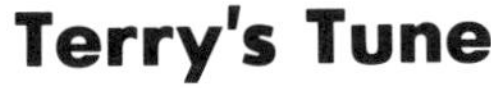

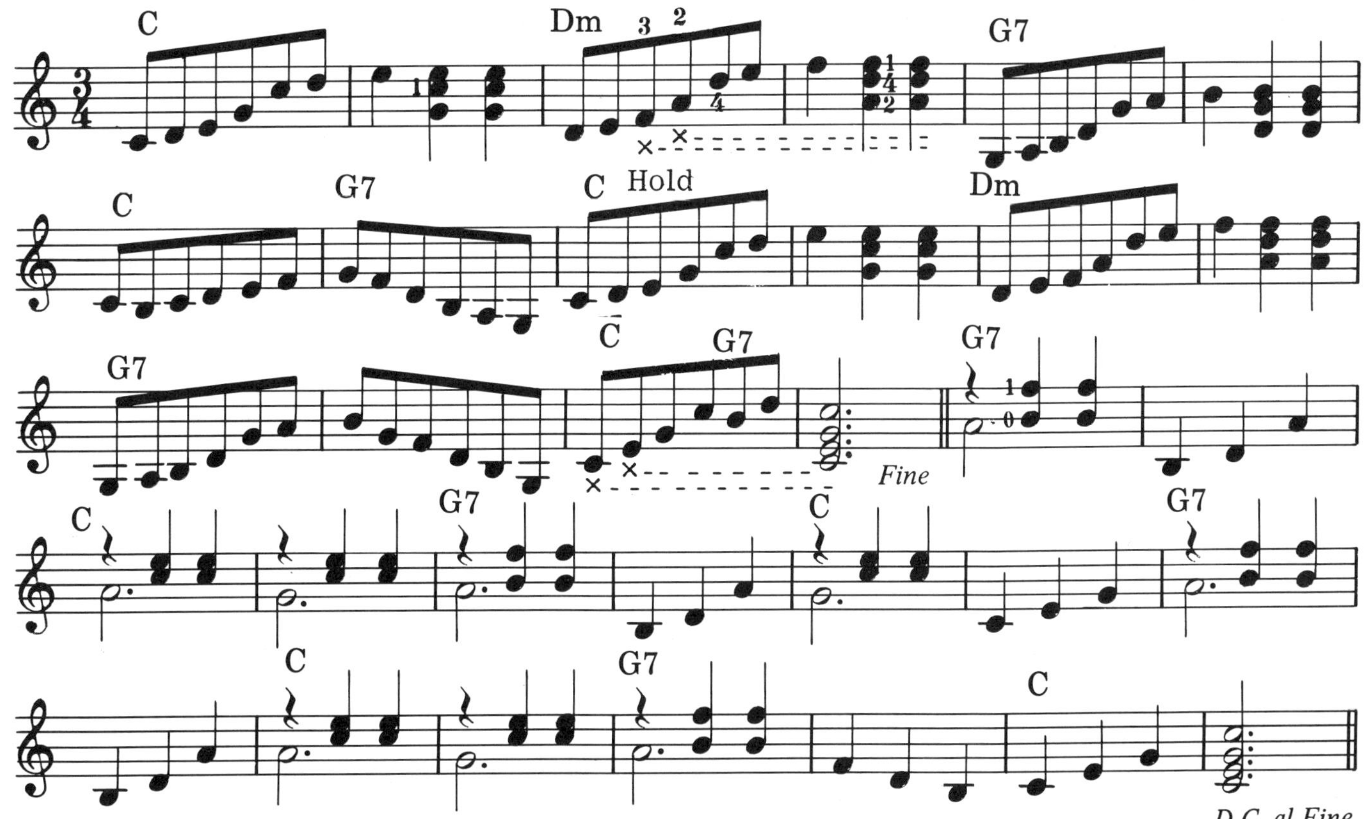

THE KEY OF G

The Key of G will have one sharp (F♯):
It will be identified by this signature:

The F-notes will be played as shown:

THE G SCALE

Note that in order to have the half-steps falling between the seventh and eighth degrees of the scale the F must be sharped.

Our major scale pattern is then correct.
(1, 1, ½, 1, 1, 1, ½.) (STEPS)

TWO-FOUR TIME

THIS SIGN  INDICATES TWO-FOUR TIME

2 — BEATS PER MEASURE
4 — A QUARTER NOTE RECEIVES ONE BEAT

TWO-FOUR time will have two beats per measure with the quarter note receiving one beat.

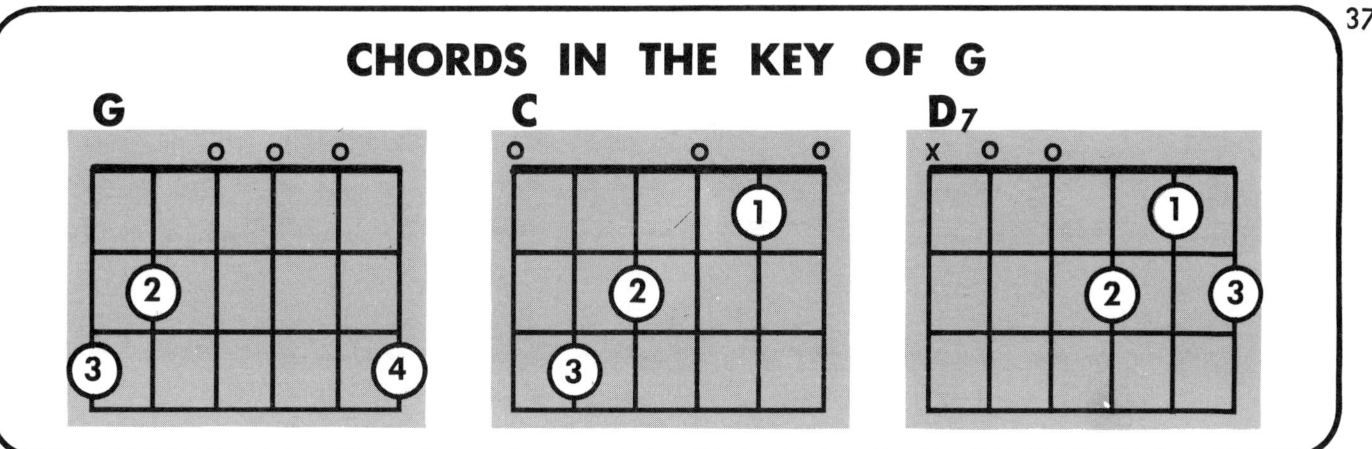

Accompaniment Styles In The Key Of G

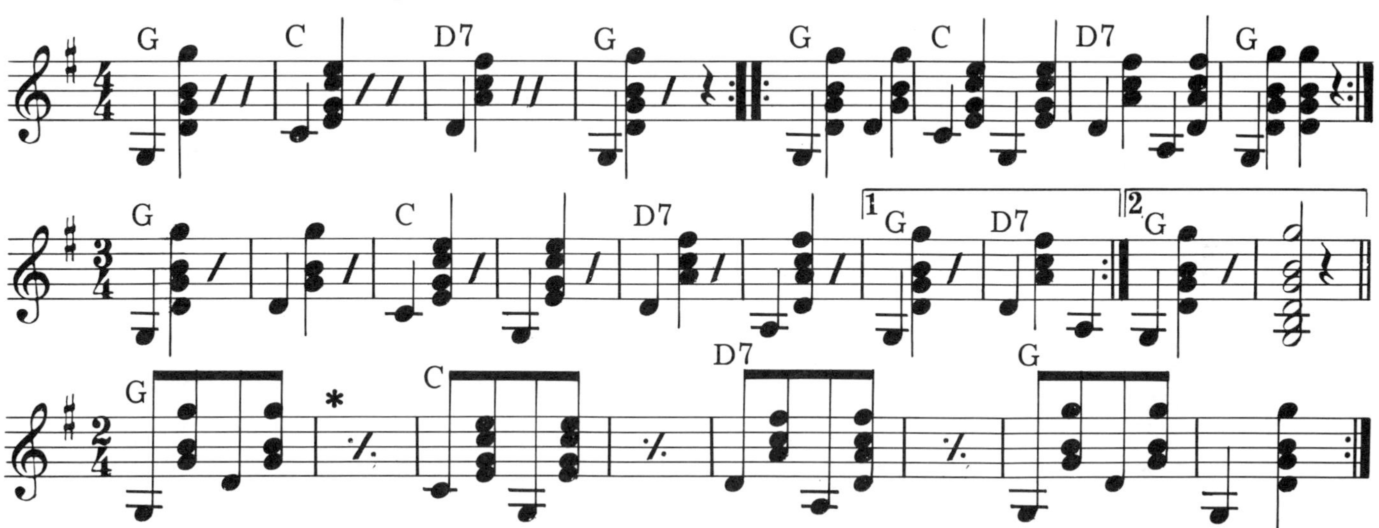

*This sign(⁒)indicates that the previous measure is to be repeated.

The following Etude introduces the notes D and B being played together. This is done by playing the note D with the first finger on the third fret of the second string and playing the note B with the second finger upon the fourth fret of the THIRD STRING.

Etude

The Old Mill

GUITAR DUET

Moderato

Arr. by Mel Bay

I

II

Fine

D.C. al Fine

A Scale Study

Count: 1 2 & 3 & 4 &

Repeat

A Serenade

GUITAR SOLO

Moderato

MEL BAY

Austrian Hymn

GUITAR DUET

HAYDN
Arr. by Mel Bay

Andante

I
II

I
II

I
II

> = Accent.

Home On The Range

GUITAR SOLO

Arr. by Mel Bay

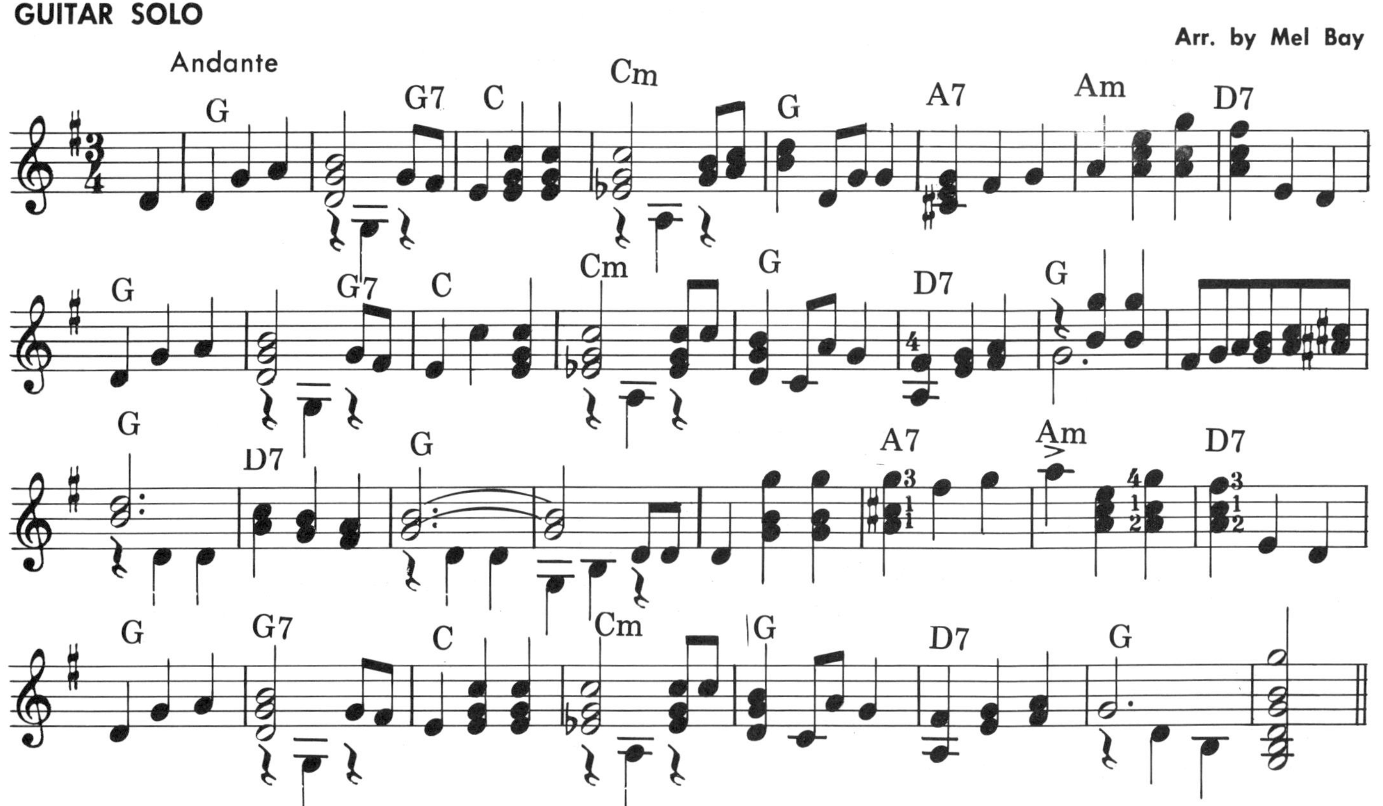

The Little Prince

GUITAR DUET

MAZAS,
Arr. by Mel Bay

Andante

I
II

Carry Me Back To Old Virginny

GUITAR SOLO

BLAND
Arr. by Mel Bay

*The wavy line before the last chord means to glide the pick slowly over the strings producing a harp-like effect. The musical term for this is QUASI ARPI.

THE KEY OF E MINOR

(Relative to G Major)

The Key of E Minor will have the same key signature as G Major.

Two E Minor Scales

The above scales should be memorized.

THE CHORDS IN THE KEY OF E MINOR

The Chords in the Key of E Minor are:

Em

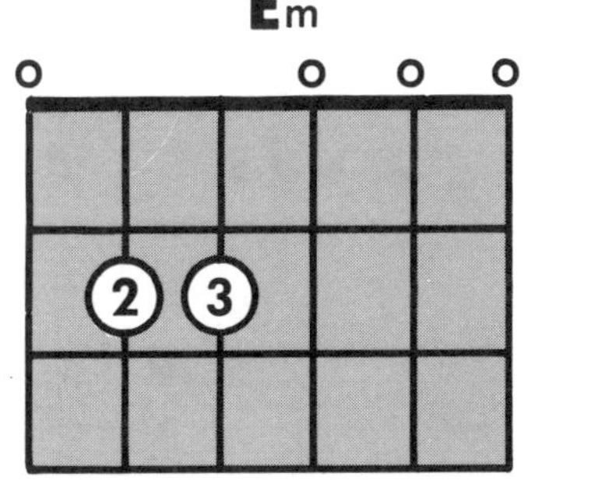

Am

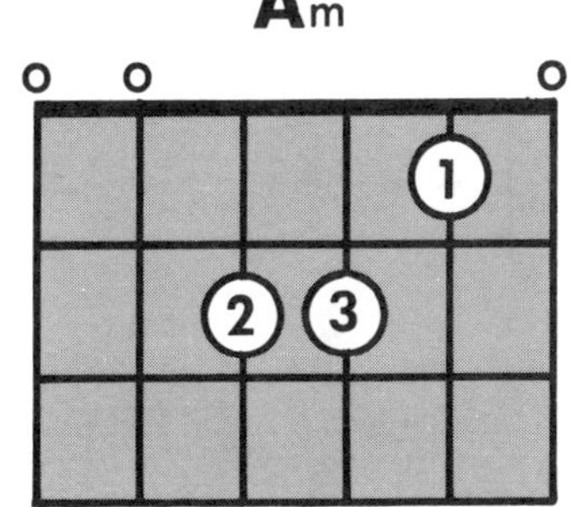

B7

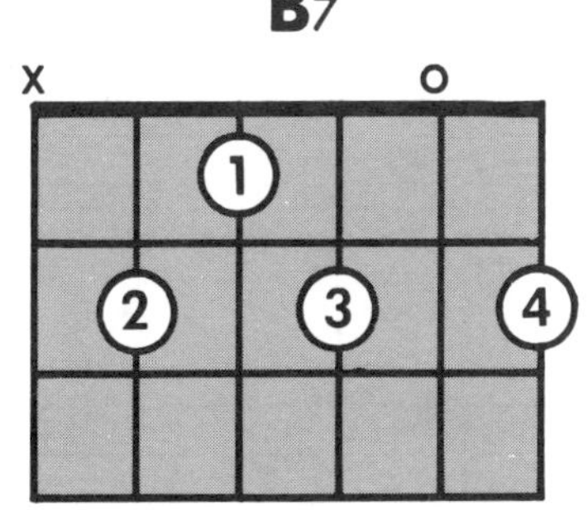

Accompaniment Styles In The Key Of E Minor

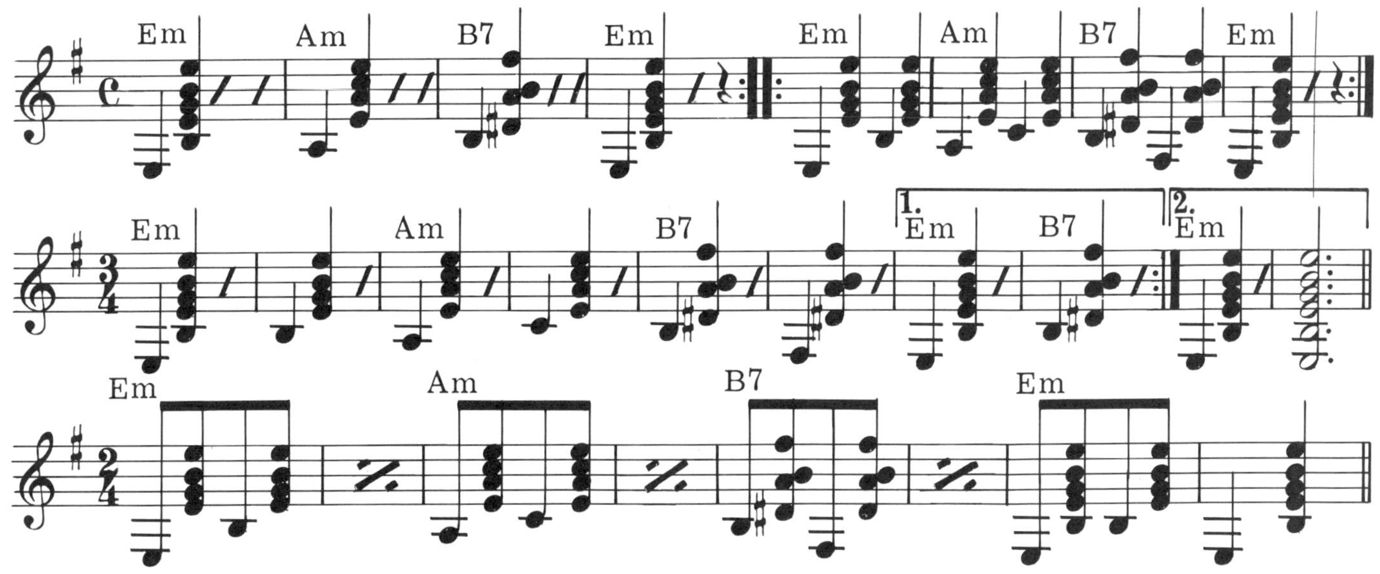

Orchestration Styles

G C D7 G B7 Em Am B7 Em

Black is the Color of My True Love's Hair

Cindy

Night Song

Sor — Bav

A CHORD REVIEW

The key of C has six chords. They are C, F, G7, Am, Dm, and E7.
The latter three are in the relative minor key but use the key signature of C.

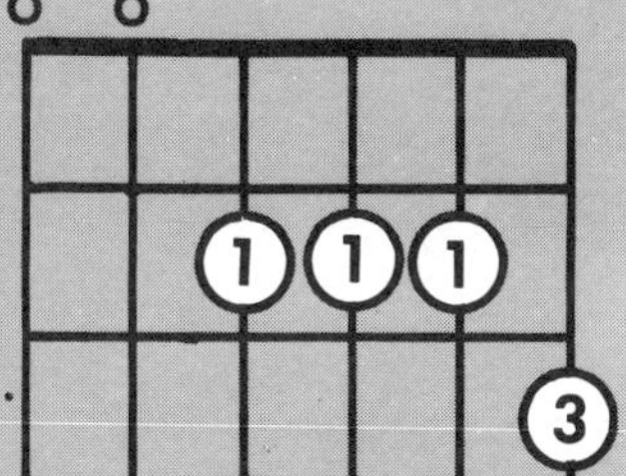

All "outside" chords are ACCIDENTAL CHORDS.
The most commonly used of these chords are D7, and A7.
The six chords found in the key of G are G, C, D7, Em, Am, and B7.
The most common accidental chords found in the key of G are A7 and E7.

Spotting the accidentals in the various chords will facilitate the reading of them . . . for example:

B7 will have a D#
E7 will have a G#
A7 will have a C#
D7 will have a F#

In the following studies you will see how they appear.

Lament

GUITAR SOLO
Slow

MEL BAY

Maytime

GUITAR DUET

WANHALL-BAY

TONE

Music is composed of sounds pleasant to the ear.

SOUND may be made from NOISE or TONE.

NOISE is made by **irregular vibrations** such as would be caused by striking a table with a hammer, the shot of a gun, or slapping two stones together.

TONE is produced by **regular vibrations** as would be caused by drawing a bow over the strings of a violin, striking the strings of a guitar, or blowing through a wind instrument, such as a trumpet.

A TONE has four characteristics . . . PITCH, DURATION, DYNAMICS and TIMBRE.

PITCH: The highness or lowness of a tone.

DURATION: The length of a tone.

DYNAMICS The force or power of a tone. (Loudness or softness).

TIMBRE: Quality of the tone.

A NOTE represents the PITCH AND DURATION of a tone.

DYNAMICS are indicated by words such as . . .

Pianissimo .... (*pp*) .... Very soft
Piano .... (*p*) .... Soft
Mezzo piano .... (*mp*)..................... Medium soft
Mezzo forte .... (*mf*).................... Medium loud
Forte .... (*f*) .... Very loud

TIMBRE depends upon the skill of the performer plus the quality of the instrument on which he is playing.

Rondo

GUITAR DUET

MAZAS, Op. 85
Arr. by Mel Bay

Allegro

Student should play both parts

Sor's Waltz

Arr. by Mel Bay

(Hold)

Bluegrass Waltz

Running the Thirds in G

A Little Bit of Hanon

Southern Fried

This is to certify that

____
STUDENT'S NAME

has now completed Mel Bay's Modern Guitar Method-Grade 1 and is now ready to enter Mel Bay's Modern Guitar Method-Grade 2.

____
TEACHER'S NAME

____
DATE